"These aren't some words on a page; lived. Possible. Proven. These are words lived out that are literally changing the world from the inside out. The family you want is possible—and this is the book you need."

Ann Voskamp, *New York Times* bestselling author
of *The Broken Way* and *One Thousand Gifts*

"In a world where it is countercultural to raise our children to live outward and not inward, Kristen Welch spurs us on in this journey of living openhearted to all that God wants to do through us. She isn't just telling us how; she is showing us by the very life her family is living today! As you read these pages, you will not only find guidance in raising children who are world changers, but you will find yourself moved to be a world changer as well!"

Ruth Schwenk, founder of TheBetterMom.com;
author of *Pressing Pause* and *For Better or for Kids*

"*Raising World Changers in a Changing World* gets to the heart of everything I have lived and believed through all the years of my ministry. Learn how to leave a legacy of faith and purpose for your children that will transform your life and theirs. Please read this book. Your life will be changed."

Sally Clarkson, author of *The Lifegiving Home*,
The Lifegiving Table, and more

"Overwhelmed. That's how I feel when I hear stories of starvation and suffering in other parts of the world. If I'm honest, I see suffering in my own city. It's here too. Homelessness, broken homes, addiction. Most of us ask the same question—What can I do?—with a fair degree of frustration.

"If you feel overwhelmed too, get ready to be encouraged. Kristen Welch answers this and many other big-picture questions about our world in her new book, *Raising World Changers in a Changing World*. Through consistently pointing parents back to the Bible and offering practical ways we can live generously where we are right now, Welch offers parents two things that are sorely lacking in our world today: hope and direction.

"You can live generously right where you are. Every family needs this life-changing book!"

Heidi St. John, author, speaker, blogger,
and executive director at Firmly Planted Family

"*Raising World Changers in a Changing World* is a must-read for every Christian parent who desires for their children to burst out of the safe, predictable bubble of the American Dream and begin living a life of service that is greater than anything they could ever ask or imagine."

Erin Odom, author of *More Than Just Making It*
and *You Can Stay Home with Your Kids*;
creator of thehumbledhomemaker.com

Raising
WORLD
CHANGERS
in a
CHANGING
WORLD

Raising
WORLD CHANGERS
in a
CHANGING WORLD

How One Family Discovered the
Beauty of Sacrifice and the Joy of Giving

KRISTEN WELCH

BakerBooks

a division of Baker Publishing Group
Grand Rapids, Michigan

Published by Baker Books
a division of Baker Publishing Group
PO Box 6287, Grand Rapids, MI 49516-6287
www.bakerbooks.com

Printed in the United States of America

Library of Congress Cataloging-in-Publication Data
Names: Welch, Kristen, 1972– author.
Title: Raising world changers in a changing world : how one family discovered the beauty of sacrifice and the joy of giving / Kristen Welch.
Description: Grand Rapids : Baker Publishing Group, 2018.
Identifiers: LCCN 2017055212 | ISBN 9780801075797 (pbk.)
Subjects: LCSH: Parenting—Religious aspects—Christianity. | Child rearing—Religious aspects—Christianity.
Classification: LCC BV4529 .W4535 2018 | DDC 248.8/45—dc23
LC record available at https://lccn.loc.gov/2017055212

Some names and details have been changed to protect the privacy of the individuals involved.

Published in association with William K. Jensen Literary Agency, 119 Bampton Court, Eugene, Oregon 97404.

18 19 20 21 22 23 24   7 6 5 4 3 2 1

TO MY KIDS
You changed my world
and now you're changing yours.

Contents

Introduction

Our world has changed every time I turn on the TV. It seems to get a little scarier and a lot more uncertain with every passing day. Whether it's due to mass shootings, terrorist plots, racial tension, or extreme weather, on some days it feels like the sky may actually be falling. But even on cloudless days it is an intimidating and daunting time to raise children in our changing world.

We have a choice: we can let the world change us, or we can change the world.

When my husband and I were handed our pink and blue bundles of joy, we didn't plan to raise world changers. But the moment we started teaching them to put others first, we discovered that small acts of kindness and compassion *do* change the world. Mostly, however, they change us.

Honestly, our lives today look nothing like I thought they would. I spent the first half of my married life trying to create a happier life for my family. But instead of feeling satisfied with all that filled our home and hearts, we felt hollow and empty. When we began giving to others, we discovered that we didn't have less for ourselves, we had more. So, yes, our lives are different than I planned—*they are better.*

This book is about finding the profound and complete joy that comes from sacrificially sharing what we have been given—our time, talents, and wallets—with those who have less. It's about living sacrificially in front of our kids and accepting the hard truth Jesus teaches: our abundance isn't for us to keep. It is given to us *to be given away.* When we follow Jesus in this way, we discover the unfathomable satisfaction, soul-quenching purpose, and unparalleled contentment that come when we give our lives away.

Parenting in a changing world changes us. My family has witnessed this firsthand. We are learning what matters and what doesn't. We teach our kids that giving doesn't make us poor, but it does cost us. Mother Teresa once said, "You must give what will cost you something. This is giving not just what you can live without, but what you can't live without, or don't want to live without. . . . Then your gift becomes a sacrifice, which will have value before God. This giving until it hurts—this sacrifice—is what I call love in action."[1] This kind of love-driven giving has a high cost, but we keep paying it because the value we receive is higher.

God's divine will is for us to be generous and for us to raise givers. But sometimes the space between his sovereign plan for our lives on the one hand and the redemption of our problems, our pain, and the wayward path we choose on the other hand is difficult to comprehend. It's much easier to trace the redemptive thread he weaves through the seasons of our lives once we've lived them. In the uncertain times living with joy is often discovered not in our gains but in what we give away. We find we are helped when we stop to help others. There is a deep, abiding, secret joy in sharing the kingdom of heaven.

In the pages of this book we will take a closer look at the life stories of modern-day givers as we address the following issues and their place in our homes: the sovereignty of God, timing, redemption, brave generosity, and how God often uses our discomfort to draw people to him.

We will also talk about joy. If we polled parents across North America most would probably say their number-one goal for their children is to be successful and happy. But the actor Jim Carrey, who has been described as both, says, "I think everybody should get rich and famous and do everything they ever dreamed of so they can see that it's not the answer."[2] Sustainable joy is found in this truth: "There is more happiness in giving than in receiving" (Acts 20:35 GNT).

In this book we will also talk about our personal motivations for this kind of living and how God has established eternity with rewards in mind. At the end of every chapter are helpful conversation starters in the form of questions that my kids will take turns answering. Hopefully this will offer some perspective on growing up in this culture—the obstacles and challenges and how they find joy in giving.

The book you hold in your hands is filled with personal, holy, and breathtaking stories of brokenhearted kingdom hunters who have impacted our family's story. They met Jesus face-to-face in the middle of their giving, and it made them want to give their lives away too. We join them in discovering the secret to true joy: giving *is receiving*.

Perhaps the most powerful lesson we teach our children is that their unique places and positions in life are not for their convenience; they are for God's glory. David Platt puts it like this: "The most glorious reason you exist is for the proclamation of the glory of God to the ends of the world. And it's more than having a nice life."[3]

This book will not offer quick fixes or easy answers in our unstable world. But if you're hunting for more joy in our changing world and deep-seated, unparalleled joy in your home that isn't dependent on culture, class, or chaos, the pages of this book are a good place to start.

Raising kids to be generous with their time, abilities, and even their small resources builds deep-rooted character. Isn't our goal to establish in them an unshakable foundation that cannot be swayed in a shifting world? Character building through the filter of giving teaches our kids the beauty of sacrifice, the value of hard work, the peace in pursuing God's glory, and the joy of putting others first. This is our purpose. This is what keeps us living and giving in a changing world.

1

The Question
We Must Ask

We are most alive when we are loving and actively giving
ourselves because we were made to do these things.

Francis Chan

I stretched out my legs on the lush, green grass and let the sun
warm me. July in Kenya is cold. I closed my eyes and took a deep
breath. It was almost as though I sensed that this moment—right
now, right here—needed to be treasured.

I'm not sure how long I sat there like that, eyes closed,
head tilted toward the African sky, listening to babies cooing
and toddlers giggling around me. *I am listening to miracles*,
I thought.

I opened my eyes to a chubby hand offering me a flower
from the nearby bush. I accepted the fragrant gift and tickled
the little girl offering it. She plopped down onto my lap, and I

looked up to see her teen mother, Veronica, finishing her lunch on a nearby blanket. She was sitting with my oldest daughter, Madison, fourteen years old at the time. They were talking.

It looked like just another Thursday in Africa. But it was more. It was holy ground. The wind whipped through the trees and blew petals from the flowering plants as if nature itself bowed down in holy reverence at what God had done through our weak and inadequate yes to his leading.

My family started Mercy House in 2010. Mercy House exists to engage, empower, and disciple women around the globe in Jesus's name: engage those with resources to say yes to relieving the plight of women in poverty, empower women and teenage mothers around the world through partnerships and sustainable fair-trade product development, and disciple women to be lifelong followers of Jesus Christ.

My family was visiting our flagship ministry in Kenya, our maternity home, where our staff rescues the most at-risk pregnant girls in the country.

I looked up from the little girl in my lap and looked over at my daughter, still deep in conversation with Veronica. The wind carried their words, and I caught bits and pieces of their conversation. I noticed they were holding hands, and I couldn't help but smile at the view.

But then there it was—the moment that changed everything. I froze when I heard Veronica ask Madison this question: "Why do you think I was born here in Kenya and you were born in America?"

I watched as my daughter chewed her lip, considering the question and how she would answer it. I couldn't stop the tears from filling my eyes. You see, you have to know Veronica's story to understand the magnitude of her question.

16

I hugged Veronica's little girl, who was still sitting in my lap, as I recalled the horrible details of her mother's life. Veronica was thirteen or fourteen years old when she came to the maternity home, but no one knew her exact age because she didn't know her own birthday. She was an orphan, and she came to us directly from a hospital in Nairobi, Kenya, where she had lived for several months as she recovered from being burned on over 40 percent of her body. While she was in a coma the medical team discovered she was pregnant. The local newspaper shared her story and how justice was being pursued for the crime against her. The article ended with a plea for someone—anyone—to help Veronica. Mercy House answered that call.

I'll never forget the day our staff in Kenya told me the details of the violent acts committed against Veronica. A distant relative had taken her in, not as a daughter but as an indentured servant. Instead of going to school with the other kids in the home, she worked. One day she was accused of stealing what would be equivalent to five dollars. Her relative tied her up, put her on the thatched roof of a small hut nearby, doused her with fuel, and set her on fire.

When these details were relayed to me I put my head down on my desk and cried. I wept for Veronica because I didn't know if anyone else had. She had experienced unspeakable hell in her short years on earth.

Within a few months at the maternity home, where she was carried from room to room by the other teen moms, we raised $10,000 so doctors could complete the surgeries that would allow her to walk again. Veronica was a fighter. She not only relearned how to walk and run but also learned to spell her name, read, and be a mother.

That's the girl who was asking my daughter the question on the grass that day.

"I don't know," Madison said after a long pause. I could tell she was thinking. It was an impossible question to answer because there was so much more behind it. Veronica might as well have asked, "Why have I known a life of suffering? Why has my life been so hard? Why does your life seem so easy compared to mine?"

Like most who have never left third-world and developing countries, these Kenyan girls know of America only from the news and movies. Generally, we are the only Americans they interact with. And while they may never visit our country, they long to because they understand how much we have. They know how much we've been given.

My daughter's story probably isn't very different from your kids' stories. She's never missed a meal or been refused school. She has free time and can use her babysitting money for trips to the mall. She's never prostituted for food. She's never been assaulted. She has loving parents and extended family. She lives in a nice house, not too big or too small. Madison has grown up in America.

Madison was ten years old when we started Mercy House. She was ten years old on her first trip to Africa. She was ten years old when we decided to give our lives away. She was ten years old when we decided it was better to give than to receive.

Over the next few years she watched us as our home was turned upside down, or maybe it was really turned right side up. Instead of living for ourselves, we started giving to others. Instead of focusing on what we wanted, we looked for ways to serve.

With anything that changes its course, there is pain and difficulty and a stretching of all things comfortable. So, yes, it was hard for our family to find a new normal, and we struggled to find a balance. But I like to think Madison's next words to Veronica came from the fertile ground in which we had raised her. I like to think that generosity had taken deep root and produced the joy of giving.

My fourteen-year-old daughter continued to answer the question posed by her African-born friend: "Maybe I was born in America and you were born here because I'm supposed to help you."

They grabbed each other's hands and held tightly: two girls from two different sides of the globe figuring out a profound truth that most of the world cannot seem to grasp. I swallowed the lump in my throat because, yes, this was it. This was the perfect answer to Veronica's question. The honesty and purity of one child's words to another were sacred.

The book *Revolution in World Mission* by K. P. Yohannan, founder of Gospel for Asia, revolutionized my life and the way I parent. He urged every North American Christian to ask themselves two questions—two questions that were answered on that lush lawn in Kenya that day.

1. Why do you think God has allowed you to be born in North America . . . and to be blessed with such material and spiritual abundance?
2. In light of the superabundance you enjoy, what do you think is your minimal responsibility to the untold millions of lost and suffering in the world?[1]

These are the questions that keep me awake at night. These are the questions that have shaped my home and turned my family right side up. I want to spend my life answering them.

I want my children to answer them with how they choose to live and give.

Go ahead. Ask yourself these questions. Where you live is not an accident; it is not the luck of the draw. There is a reason you are where you are. God has a purpose for placing you here and not there. What do you think that purpose is?

I don't think it's a mathematical mistake that one-third of the world is rich enough to ease the burden of the other two-thirds, who are desperately poor and living on less than one dollar per day. Nor is it a curious coincidence that we are already sitting on the answer: we are supposed to help each other. It's something we teach our children from the cradle. It's called sharing. We have more than enough, and we have enough to share. It sounds like a match made in heaven. Maybe it was God's plan all along for us to love others and, instead of accumulating more stuff, to give some of what we have away.

America is a land of opportunity. It's a place where we can achieve all we want and more. But just because we can get more, should we? It's a hard question only we can answer. This isn't about the size of a home or a car or a bank account. It's not about guilt or lifestyle—it's about the size of our hearts.

I know people who have much and give much. I know people who have almost nothing and give even more.

Yohannan challenges us with more tough questions in *No Longer a Slumdog*. He asks, "How many more cars, clothes, toys and trinkets do we really need before we wake up and realize that half the world goes to bed every night with empty stomachs and naked bodies?"[2]

I believe when God asks us what we did with our talents, our resources, our land-of-the-free, home-of-the-brave opportunities, we will be accountable for our answers. We may give already. But we have been given so much. We could give more, share more, and do more. Not to prove we are good people or because we need a longer list of good works. We give because our purpose is to glorify God. We give because he first loved us, and we are to love others. We give because we have it to give. We give because we want to raise children who give. We want to see our kids change someone else's world.

Maybe this is why we have so much. Maybe this is why we were born where we were born. Maybe this is why we are where we are today. I don't know where you are right now. You might be in any country in the world. You might be in the middle of your house in the middle of suburbia folding laundry. You might be reading this on your shift break at your job in the hospital on floor two. You might be standing in line at the pharmacy, waiting for a prescription for your mother, who is very sick. You might be in the lowest season of your life or in the best. I don't know. But I believe where you are matters. I believe we are where we are for a reason. And we simply must acknowledge that God in all his power and sovereignty placed us among the world's richest people for a purpose other than fulfilling the American dream.

Someone in your world, at your job, in your neighborhood, or on your path needs to know that you are where you are because you can help them where they are. Someone is waiting for you to share your money, your time, or your life with them. We were created to reveal the glory of Jesus to others.

You might question where God has you today. Why here, God? Why this hard, broken place? I have thought about my daughter's words many times. They remind me of my purpose. I was created for more than surviving, getting by, or moving to the next phase in life. When our hands are busy serving others, we aren't thinking about what we don't have. Instead, we are reminded about what we do have. We were created for more than filling our time and our lives with more stuff and more space. We were created for a purpose and to live our lives with purpose. We were created to give our lives away.

What we choose to give is not as important as our motive for giving it. If we give with good and generous hearts we will give our best. And God honors that.

We change the world when we change another person's day, one small act at a time. And when we change the world for someone else, we change it for ourselves too. I want to raise children who ask hard questions of themselves. I want my kids to press into who they are, what they have, and what they are supposed to do with what they've been given. When we are obedient enough to ask hard questions and brave enough to encourage our kids to do the same, we unlock a deep well of joy. This kind of joy isn't touched by our circumstances or what we receive in life. This kind of unparalleled joy comes from giving our lives away.

I often think back to that day on the green, grassy lawn in Kenya. I close my eyes and remember that *one moment* when everything changed. That moment when I wanted to live out the answer my daughter had given. I'm challenged every day by the choice our family faces: we can let the world change us, or we can change the world.

Start
WORLD-CHANGING
CONVERSATIONS
with Your Kids

Each chapter ends with one of my family members answering relevant questions that can serve as conversation starters with the kids under your roof. I asked my daughter Madison to answer the following questions. I hope they lead to good conversations with your kids.

1. What do you think being a world changer means? I think being a world changer means doing what you can to change the world right where you are. It doesn't mean starting a movement or moving to a third-world country; being a world changer is about small acts of kindness and changing the world around you in small, tangible ways. Whether it's offering a smile to a stranger, starting a conversation about your faith, being a friend to a nonbeliever, or any number of other kind acts, you are being a world changer to the people all around you.

2. Do you think God puts us in certain places for specific reasons? When I think back to my conversation with Veronica that day at Mercy House, I am hit with a flood of memories. I remember the first time I met Veronica and the compassion I felt for a girl just a bit older than I was. She was sweet and caring and very curious. I remember her asking me many questions about my life. But I was taken aback when she asked me about why I was born in America and she was born in

Africa. I responded in the best way I knew how and just let God take the conversation. I absolutely believe that he put me in that moment with sweet Veronica for a reason. Whether it was for the purpose of simply setting her heart at ease or a step in her transformation, I will never know; however, God knows, and he used that small moment for his glory. God absolutely puts us in certain places for specific reasons. Where we are, right now, is the place that God has put us, and he can use us in unimaginable ways for his purpose and his glory.

3. How do you think kids can "give their lives away"? I think kids can give their lives away by simply asking God to use them to further his kingdom and by giving their lives fully and completely over to him. By giving God 100 percent, we are surrendering our lives to him and letting his purpose take control. It definitely won't be easy, and there will surely be some awkward and uncomfortable moments (trust me, I've had quite a few!), but living for God isn't supposed to be easy. Don't worry or back away from fulfilling God's purpose in your life because you feel as though you aren't good enough or because you're just a kid. God uses kids and people who aren't good enough every day, all over the world. I mean, I'm sitting here writing this as a seventeen-year-old with no special qualifications or skills, and yet God is using my shortcomings and my life for his purpose.

4. Do you have any advice for other kids who are tempted to let the world change them? In all honesty, I've been tempted and have given into letting the world change me. Rather than listen to what God was calling me to do, I've taken the easier road so that

I wouldn't have to feel uncomfortable or look weird. I am often reminded of the story of Jonah, who resisted God's calling for his life and let the world change him by taking the easier way out. But the world's idea of the easier way out isn't always in our best interest. However, God rescued Jonah in the form of a fish, and Jonah ended up fulfilling God's purpose even though he resisted at first. Don't let it take a big fish for you to fulfill God's purpose for your life. Though it may seem tough to resist the temptation of letting the world change you, God is faithful and he will never let you be tempted beyond what you can handle. Let a God who loves you, cares for you, and has your best interest at heart guide your life and not the world.

Practice
GENEROSITY

- Play the "What do we have extra?" game. Read Luke 12:13–21 together. Source: http://www.kidsofintegrity .com/lessons/generosity/hands-options/what-do-we -have-extra-game.

- Pick a project. Have a family fund-raiser (for example, garage sale, bake sale, lemonade stand) and raise money to give away.

2

Jesus

The Greatest Giver Who Changed the World

The highest act of love is the giving of the best gift, and,
if necessary, at the greatest cost, to the least deserving.
That's what God did.

John Piper

"Mom, I just want to kill something," my ten-year-old son said. I covered my mouth, trying not to laugh at his very serious declaration. I remember thinking this must be the testosterone surge little boys have periodically that I'd read about. Jon-Avery was in the fourth grade at the time, and it was proving to be his most challenging school year. He was doing fine academically, but socially he struggled. He's always been a nice boy, sweet and kind, sensitive and intuitive, and exactly the kind of boy that tends to be targeted by other boys.

Recess on the playground with other fourth graders who were better at football, a little faster, and a lot more aggressive was the hardest part of his day. It's the age boys go from flag football to tackle if they are serious about the sport. Jon-Avery was lean and mean on the field mentally, but his heart didn't want to hurt anyone. He discovered for the first time that he wasn't fitting in and that kids could be very mean.

In just a matter of months our sweet, always-happy boy became discouraged, and his confidence was destroyed. It was heartbreaking to witness, and we were looking for a way to help heal his heart. When he stated he wanted to kill something, I was determined to make that happen (as crazy as it sounds). We bought him a bow-and-arrow set for Christmas, thinking hunting might bring him the dose of self-assurance he needed. Every day for hours he would shoot arrows at the target. He loved it.

One day from my bedroom window I was watching him shoot, and on a whim I decided to google "archery lessons" in my town. The search produced a coach's name. I emailed him and explained that though my son was new to archery, my husband and I thought it might be just the thing to boost his confidence.

To make a long story short, we met Coach Steve at the only range within thirty minutes from our house, and as they say, the rest is history. Jon-Avery fell head over heels in love with the sport. But not for the reason you might think. He had a natural aptitude for it and a good eye; he was disciplined and wanted to absorb everything he could. But the main reason he loved archery was Coach Steve.

Steve Overbeck was one of the most generous men I've ever met. Months turned into years as we watched this man pour into our son's life. Coach Steve had participated in Olympic trials and won many titles. Beginning in his college shooting days, he acquired a great deal of archery equipment. He constantly tweaked and changed Jon-Avery's bow, a necessity for a growing archer, as he taught him, but he did it as his sponsor. He would trade parts and pieces, saving us a lot of money, because he was first a generous person and second a coach. But we didn't love Coach Steve just because he was generous with stuff. We loved him because he didn't emphasize winning; instead he constantly whispered godly words of encouragement and praise into our son's ear. Jon-Avery began to stand taller and to shoot straighter, but mostly he began to believe in himself again.

Nearly every week I thanked God for putting this man of God in my son's life. I will never forget the day we got a call telling us that Coach Steve, still a young, lean athlete and barely fifty years old, was diagnosed with stage IV cancer. We were devastated. In the beginning he continued to teach our son and other archers as he fought courageously for his life. He endured radiation and chemotherapy and rarely missed a chance to teach kids archery. His passion for the sport and for his students seemed to triple even as he lost weight. He hid his suffering as he leaned over Jon-Avery's bow, making slight adjustments and quietly, faithfully, whispering words of passion and encouragement to our son.

A year after the diagnosis Coach Steve was too sick to come to tournaments, but he continued to coach Jon-Avery from his house over the phone. The last time Jon-Avery saw him, Coach Steve adjusted his bow on his lap in bed as he was too weak to leave it. As the end neared, Jon-Avery was at church camp, and every day we were begging God for a miracle. Watching Coach

Steve slip away and walking our son through it was one of the most difficult parenting experiences of my life.

Jon-Avery wanted to see him one more time, but his wife thought it would be better for Jon-Avery's last memory to be a happier one since Coach Steve's body had changed so dramatically.

"Mom, there's still so much I want to say to him. Do you think he knows how much I love him?" We cried together in the kitchen and held each other. I urged him to write a letter. We took it over to Coach Steve's house, and his seventeen-year-old son read it to his father in bed while we cried in the car.

Coach Steve died. I watched my brave child become a man as he stood in front of five hundred people at the funeral of his beloved coach and read the letter he had written to him.

I was a ten-year-old boy with a bow and arrows when I met Coach Steve, and I didn't even know I had found my passion. I didn't know that my bow would lead me to meet such an amazing, kind, and loving coach. The more I got to know you, the more I saw how much Christ's love was evident in your life. But what got my attention the most was, after being diagnosed with cancer, how much you relied on God and lived your life with purpose and gave your life away.

The longer you lived through this cancer ordeal, the more your life reminded me of Philippians 1:12–18. The passage is about how Paul was imprisoned, normally a bad occurrence, and how good still came from it. Because he was in prison, guards and prisoners came to know about Christ. Even though Paul's circumstances changed, his purpose hadn't. It was just a change of mission fields.

You were diagnosed with cancer, but good is still coming from it. Every time I shoot an arrow, I am reminded of Christ's love that has been shown to me through you. You've taught me three lessons:

1. The closer you get to death, the more alive you should become in Christ.
2. Being generous is so much more fulfilling than receiving things.
3. Trials bring you closer to God.

I can't tell you how much I love you.

Months after Coach Steve's death Jon-Avery didn't cry as much, but a heavy cloud of grief clung to him. He still hadn't picked up his bow to shoot a single arrow. His love for the sport was so tightly wrapped up in his love for his coach that he didn't know if he would ever shoot again. Just walking into the backyard and seeing the large target bale Coach Steve had given him was enough to send him away in tears. Although he was now thirteen we got a glimpse of that lost little ten-year-old boy again, and it broke our hearts.

About ten months after Coach Steve's passing we got an unexpected call from Frannie, his widow. Frannie asked if she could come over and give something to Jon-Avery for his fourteenth birthday. She and her son sat in our living room, and we talked about the hole Steve's absence had left in our hearts.

Then Frannie brought in Coach Steve's most prized archery possession: his custom, high-tech, Olympic-style recurve bow. She said, "Jon-Avery, you were special to Coach Steve. He left a note and wanted you to have his bow." There wasn't a dry eye in our house. It's one of those moments our family will never forget.

Even after his death Coach Steve's wild generosity was blessing our family and impacting our son. But mostly, this man—his memory and the legacy he left—was still pointing us to Jesus. Jesus is the greatest giver of all. He became the ultimate gift. Isn't seeing our kids discover who Christ is our greatest desire as parents? Our world is changing faster than we can blink, not because we are discovering better ways to live but because people are searching for and seeking purpose. Our culture is looking for satisfaction, and we will try just about anything and turn everything on its end to find it.

In the beginning, on that very first day when God created, he gave. He gave us the earth and everything in it. He created plants and animals and people and declared it was very good. He said we could have it all except for one tree. But we wanted more. From the foundation of the world, we see a God who is wildly generous. When we took the one thing that didn't belong to us, God gave us more—his Son. "Great love begins with great giving."[1] We see the ultimate gift of love played out in John 3:16: "For God so loved the world that he gave his one and only Son" (NIV).

Jesus came wrapped in humanity and became the greatest example of generosity because he gave the greatest gift—himself. The night Jesus gave his life, he told his disciples, "Greater love has no one than this: to lay down one's life for one's friends" (John 15:13 NIV).

As parents we get a small glimpse into this kind of sacrificial love. We would do anything for our children—even find something for them to kill. But only God freely gave a Son who came willingly to die.

32

I love reading Max Lucado. He has a way with words like no one else. He brings down to our understanding this huge idea of deity and humanity in the form of a baby. It's tempting to save this kind of story for Christmas, but Christmas is every day for Christians. I urge you to highlight the following words, pull them out over dinner, and read them to your children. They might not comprehend every word now, but if they grow up hearing it, one day they will.

God as a fetus. Holiness sleeping in a womb. The creator of life being created.

God was given eyebrows, elbows, two kidneys, and a spleen. He stretched against the walls and floated in the amniotic fluids of his mother.

God had come near.

He came, not as a flash of light or as an unapproachable conqueror, but as one whose first cries were heard by a peasant girl and a sleepy carpenter. The hands that first held him were unmanicured, calloused, and dirty.

No silk. No ivory. No hype. No party. No hoopla.

Were it not for the shepherds, there would have been no reception. And were it not for a group of stargazers, there would have been no gifts.

Angels watched as Mary changed God's diaper. The universe watched with wonder as The Almighty learned to walk. Children played in the street with him. And had the synagogue leader in Nazareth known who was listening to his sermons. . . .

Jesus may have had pimples. He may have been tone-deaf. Perhaps a girl down the street had a crush on him or vice versa. It could be that his knees were bony. One thing's for sure: He was, while completely divine, completely human.[2]

33

Jesus came to die. He walked on earth and showed us how to live. He didn't give away money, but he freely gave healing, freedom, life, and forgiveness. And when he left he gave us three critical tasks that should shape our homes as we parent our kids. He commanded us to do the following:

1. *Love God.* "'Teacher, which command in God's Law is the most important?' Jesus said, '"Love the Lord your God with all your passion and prayer and intelligence." This is the most important, the first on any list'" (Matt. 22:36–38).
2. *Love others* (our neighbors). "But there is a second to set alongside it: 'Love others as well as you love yourself.' These two commands are pegs; everything in God's Law and the Prophets hangs from them" (Matt. 22:39–40).
3. *Make disciples.* "And Jesus came and said to them, 'All authority in heaven and on earth has been given to me. Go therefore and make disciples of all nations, baptizing them in the name of the Father and of the Son and of the Holy Spirit, teaching them to observe all that I have commanded you. And behold, I am with you always, to the end of the age'" (Matt. 28:18–20 ESV).

Jesus didn't just tell us what to do; he showed us what to do. He was our example. He honored his Father and glorified God in everything he did. He fed the hungry, clothed the poor, and healed the sick. He sought out the discouraged and disregarded and offered them hope and freedom. He made disciples. He spent time with people, built relationships with them, and required obedience from them. He was busy—he walked everywhere and worked hard. Jesus showed us how to live and give and how to pray.

He spent his time on earth serving others. Tom Nelson says:

> We are rightly in awe of Jesus, who shockingly ignores cultural convention by picking up a basin and towel and washing His disciples' dirty, stinky feet. Yet we tend to forget that Jesus had been modeling a basin-and-towel kind of servanthood in a carpentry shop for years. Jesus' humble service in the workplace was the training ground for that glorious display of servanthood in the upper room in Jerusalem.[3]

Jesus began his most famous sermon on the mountain with these words: "Blessed are the poor in spirit" (Matt. 5:3 ESV). Less than a decade ago I was a middle-class mom in a slum in Kenya, surrounded by extreme poverty for the first time but discovering that I was the one who was really poor. Seeing myself in this light helped me to see the world more clearly as John Thornton points out: "Only when we recognize our true state can we hear Jesus. We are poor. We may claim, 'I am rich; I have acquired wealth and don't need a thing,' but Jesus responds, 'You do not realize that you are wretched, pitiful, poor, blind and naked' (Rev. 3:17 NIV)."[4]

As parents we have a grave responsibility. It's up to us to lead our kids in the mandates that Jesus left us. Just as Jesus is our example, we are our children's examples. After my last book, *Raising Grateful Kids in an Entitled World*, came out, I did something I'm not entirely comfortable with—I spoke about parenting to parents. I qualified everything I said with, "I'm not an expert; I'm in the trenches just like you." But as I traveled to churches and talked with pastors and children's leaders and youth pastors, it was surprising to me how often I heard their discouragement regarding parents who left spiritual teaching and Bible education entirely up to the church. I was startled to hear one pastor say he read that the average child gets only about forty hours per year of spiritual teaching from a church, and that's with regular weekly attendance. Many mentioned that attendance wasn't a priority with the popularity of traveling sports teams, dance competitions, and school activities that took precedence over church attendance. As such, forty hours was often a generous estimate.

If we are depending on the church to raise spiritually grounded, mature believers who live out their purpose, glorify God, and withstand the shifting truth sweeping across our world, we will fail our children. The church comes alongside the family to emphasize and reiterate what children are learning at home. If we are not teaching and modeling biblical truth to our kids, their foundation may not withstand the storms of life.

How do we practically follow Jesus's example today? We do what he did.

Love God

We show our love for God not by what we say but by what we do. We make God the highest priority in our lives and in our homes. I think this was the most remarkable thing about Coach Steve. Everyone knew he loved God—not because he told them he did but because he showed them he did by how he lived.

If someone interviewed our children today and asked them, "What's the most important thing in your family?" how would they answer? If the interviewer pressed a little harder and asked, "What does your family spend the most time doing or spend the most money on?" what would our children say? Kids are honest, sometimes painfully so. They are superb at calling our bluffs and seeing our motives. They also delight us when they catch us doing something right.

When Emerson, my youngest, asked me what this book was about (as I was writing it), I answered, "It's a book about generosity and how we've learned it's better to give than to receive." She laughed! "But Mom, I'm not generous. I don't have any money!"

I thought to myself, *There goes that idea*, and laughed with her. But I thought about her words and decided I needed to explain further. "Honey, we can and should be generous with our money. But it's more than that. You spent all morning volunteering at Mercy House, we are cleaning your room so you can share it with someone who needs a place to stay tonight, and you have been driving me crazy about completing the paperwork so we can offer respite to foster-care families. This is living a generous life."

She replied, "Oh, well, I thought that was just loving God."

Boom! It's both.

Love Others

We love our neighbors in our world by seeing their needs and meeting them. This is practical, real-time need generosity. This is taking what we have and sharing it with those who have less, not in theory but in feet-on-the-street, tangible acts of love. I think Coach Steve modeled this perfectly. He had his own family but took time to use his gift for a hobby he loved as a way to pour into kids who needed encouragement. Generosity isn't just giving stuff. It's also giving ourselves.

That being said, it is giving material things too. It doesn't get any easier to understand than this:

What I'm interested in seeing you do is:
sharing your food with the hungry,
inviting the homeless poor into your homes,
putting clothes on the shivering ill-clad,
being available to your own families.
Do this and the lights will turn on,
and your lives will turn around at once.
Your righteousness will pave your way. (Isa.
58:7–8)

We have good friends who lead the American office of Vision Rescue, a beautiful ministry that provides hope in the streets of Mumbai, India. One of their projects is converting old school buses into mobile classrooms to educate the huge population of street kids. Our friends have four daughters who decided to have a garage sale to raise the $2,400 it costs to pay a school-teacher's salary. I told my kids about it, and we gathered some things for their sale. They spent weeks collecting and pricing items. They held a giant sale and lived out an incredible story of loving others. God multiplied their efforts, and they raised $40,051, enough to pay the salary for sixteen teachers! I want my family to be a part of as many of these kinds of stories as possible.

Make Disciples

In my opinion making disciples is the number one failure of the church as a whole. We are excellent at evangelism—we are strong go-ers. But we are weak stay-ers. If we follow Jesus's example we make disciples in two ways: relationship and obedience. We become a bridge to the lost with our lives.

38

I've shared with you how an archery coach discipled our son through relationship. It's the second method, obedience, that is often missing from our lives. My husband, Terrell, and Jon-Avery have their own Discovery Bible Study each week, just the two of them, talking about father/son things and the struggles young and older men face. Guy stuff. Discovery Bible Study involves reading a passage of Scripture aloud in a group or with your family, writing it down verse by verse, sharing your thoughts on what you think the passage is saying, and then making an "I will" statement of obedience. For example, John 3:16 is about God loving the world so much that he gave his only Son to save us and offer us eternal life. My statement might be, "This week I will tell someone that Jesus died for them because he loves them." Those in my group will hold me accountable and ask me whom I told the next time we meet. Simple. Profound. (Other examples might be "I will acknowledge that God is the only giver of eternal life." "I will share with 'James' that God sacrificed his Son to reach the world.") The beauty of Discovery Bible Study is that you don't have to share the plan of salvation or make a convert out of the person you speak to. Just share what God taught you through the passage you studied.

Generous Faith

When I picked up my son one day from the archery range where he goes several times a week to shoot his bow, he told me he shared the weekly Scripture passage he and his dad had studied with another archer, a middle-aged man who just happened to be the best in his division in Texas. They had become friends on the shooting line over the previous few months. "I think I left him speechless," Jon-Avery said. I don't know if this man will ever follow Jesus, but he has a good chance with my son on his heels. I told Jon-Avery I was proud of him for being generous with his faith. This is how we make disciples.

Jon-Avery started shooting again with Coach Steve's archery equipment. "I think he would want me to shoot for him," he said. I swallowed the giant lump in my throat. It took some time for him to climb back to where he had been. But just a few months after he started shooting again he asked if he could do high school online from home so that he could shoot up to two hundred arrows a day. He wants to shoot in college, and who knows where his passion will take him.

A sweet friend of ours who was going through a painful divorce commented one day that her eleven-year-old son, who was struggling with the changes in his family, was interested in archery. Jon-Avery overheard her and asked if he could give this boy lessons—for free. Jon-Avery had saved his money and bought a training bow so he could offer lessons to boys who might need a little extra encouragement as he had. He was following Coach Steve's example of generosity because Coach Steve had followed Jesus's example.

God reminded me that our relationship with Coach Steve was never really about archery for our family. It was about being receivers who learn how to be givers. It was about being like Jesus. We are generous because he has been generous to us.

Start
WORLD-CHANGING CONVERSATIONS
with Your Kids

I asked my son, Jon-Avery, to answer the following questions. I hope they lead to good conversations with your kids.

1. What do you think it means to be generous? Can kids be generous? Generosity is not just a money thing. It is a lifestyle. It is about realizing what Jesus has done for us and letting that change us. It is about letting his sacrifice change the way we act and live and think. We have to model our lives after Jesus, fitting our schedules into his and not the other way around. Jesus is our example of generosity, so when we strive to be like him we become more generous. Generosity is also about seeing the needs around us and using what God has given us as a way to share about him. The things God has given us are just tools to be generous with, things we can use to share and meet needs with, all to help open doors to share the gospel. I think generosity is using what God has given us to help open doors to let us share about his Son, Jesus.

Generosity is often associated with money, but it is so much more than that. We can be generous with everything we have, however much it may be. We can be generous with our time by volunteering or giving up some free time to help someone else. We can be generous simply by meeting the needs in front of us, by loving our neighbors, by helping the person God has placed in our lives.

2. What do you think it means to live a generous life? Coach Steve gave me one of the greatest gifts anyone has ever given me. Through the way he lived his life, he allowed me to see a picture of Christ's sacrifice in a whole new light. He gave me a new perspective on the gospel and made it so much more real. As I spent more and more time with him, I realized what it meant to live a generous life. I realized that the model of generosity was God who became man and then died on this earth for our sins. Jesus was Coach Steve's model of generosity, and he illustrated a generous life so well that Jesus became my model for life. And it changed my life. For the first time the gospel became a real, living, life-changing force in and around my and others' lives.

3. Do you think sharing your faith is a way to be generous to others? Absolutely. I think that wherever we are in life can be used by God for his purposes. I have been given a passion and talent for archery. I don't know if I will do it my whole life or even where I want to go with it. But for now, I will continue to shoot because I can use it to share my faith. I think of the question that some of the religious leaders asked Jesus: "Who is our neighbor?" He then told the story of the good Samaritan and the man he found on the path. Our neighbor is the person God places in our lives, the person we find on our path. We know them and are in a position to be generous to them. If we don't share with them, perhaps no one will. Take stock of your place in life. What has God given you? What gifts or talents or positions do you have? Whom has he placed in your path? Use what God has given you and share with the people he has put on your path. It may not seem like it, but you could be instrumental in someone else's life. God has placed you around people you know who do not know him.

4. What advice would you give your parents if you could? (And you can, because your mom is asking!) Don't stop being generous. No matter how down you get, please continue to live your lives in this obedience that has shaped our family. You have been such a model of obedience and of living a life for Christ. You face real spiritual warfare and so many other struggles in what you are doing. But I want to remind you that it is worth it. I know it is hard, but you have to take it day by day. You have no idea the impact you have had on me and the rest of the family. I couldn't ask for a better life, one in which I am constantly surrounded by the wonderful chaos of ministry and changing the world. I don't think I could go back to a "normal" life. This is my new normal.

Don't stop being obedient. I know that everything you do is crazy and daunting, and it seems like it is too much or that we won't be able to do it. But every time you have said yes, God has provided. Every time we have a need it is eventually met, even if not in the way we imagined. No matter how many struggles we have, God is still with us. So the next time you feel God is telling you to do something, please say yes.

Don't stop being awesome parents. You and Dad are the best parents I could ever have. I want you to know that, even though sometimes I don't act like it. Whatever you are doing, please keep doing it and helping others do it. I know we make it really tough sometimes, but it is paying off. I love you.

Practice

GENEROSITY

- Start a tradition of giving. Make a favorite dessert or treat for you and for another family. Ask that family to fill the pan and pass it on to someone else (some say this was an unspoken Southern custom).

- Help your kids look for opportunities to teach what they love to a younger child—for example, playing an instrument or teaching a sport.

3

When There's Too Much or Not Enough to Go Around

There are people in the world so hungry that God cannot appear to them except in the form of bread.

Mahatma Gandhi

He sat at our kitchen table and told us a story about bread.

"There was a severe drought in my country. I traveled to the hardest hit regions—to the people who were starving—and everywhere I looked I saw hungry people. So many had already died. They had no bread to eat," he said with a deep sigh. "I left the drought-affected area, and the same day I got on a plane to the USA. When I arrived my host took me from the airport to a grocery store and led me to an aisle filled with fresh-baked bread. He asked me to choose the kind of bread I wanted to have with the dinner his wife was preparing. There were so many loaves—row after row of loaves of bread. I stood there for several minutes, and then I told him I could not choose. I was no longer hungry because when I closed my eyes, I could still see the starving."

I can't tell you his name or show you his picture because revealing his identity could endanger him in other parts of the world. But I can tell you that the man who sat at my kitchen table risks his life daily in dangerous places to make disciples who make disciples. Years before we met our friend, we read miraculous stories in disciple-making books of his work among Muslims and how God was using him to spread the gospel to unreached people. I cannot describe the honor it was to feed him, provide transportation while he visited our city, and listen to his stories with our kids.

It was humbling to have him sit at my kitchen table in my middle-class neighborhood where we eat all the bread we want.

I am not a generous person by nature. Just ask my daughters, who like to borrow my clothes and jewelry. Nor am I a great cook. I can follow a recipe, but I cook only because people in my house want to eat, not because I'm passionate about cooking or creative with food. I'm an introvert so people drain me. Put all these together and I'm not exactly the hostess with the mostest.

But sometimes when we do what makes us uncomfortable— such as have houseguests from around the world—our tables become altars and our kitchen rugs become holy ground and we are filled with much more than food. From what I can tell so far, I'm raising a high percentage of introverts. I want them to see me stepping out of my comfort zone, not hiding behind it, so they will have the confidence to follow in my footsteps. In that sometimes-awkward time of stretching us God also comforts us and gives us so much more than we give.

So on that Saturday when my husband showed up unexpectedly with our friend from another country, whom he had been driving around to meetings, and asked if they could stop for lunch, I said yes. Instead of running errands with my kids, I lingered around the kitchen table and listened and learned and let my children see what really matters most—*people*. On this day I wanted my kids to know that people are always more important than plans. In our culture we always have plans. Our calendars are full, and we are busy. We race from one appointment to another; we multitask and accomplish much. But I wonder if in our haste to check the next thing off our lists we sometimes miss the opportunity to connect with people.

As I imagined our friend standing in the bread aisle, my eyes filled with tears because I have met women around the world who were too hungry to see God except in the form of bread. I quietly told him about meeting desperate street mothers in one of the country's deadliest slums on the day I left Kenya. I could hardly get the words out as I remembered one mother who was curled up in a ball in the corner of the room grieving her toddler son, who had been stolen while she slept a few days prior, and another mother who had gotten pregnant again just so she could sell the second baby growing in her womb.

These were the poorest, most disregarded women—street moms who begged during the day and prostituted at night, often with a baby tied to their backs. I was invited to meet and work with these desperate women as an outreach of our maternity homes. I didn't know what to do, but I was desperate to do something.

I left that place without running water, a place you want to run from, and held my too-big sleeping children and cried in their hair, grateful I'd never had to make desperate choices to keep them alive. Two days later, I stood on a stage at the largest, most affluent megachurch in my city. I did my best to hold it together and remember who I was and *where* I was, but all I could think about was that desperate mom who was still looking for her son. I looked out at the manicured hands and the designer bags and those who have so much. Then I heard God's voice whisper, *Do not judge these women by what they have; they are the same as those who have not. They are all desperately looking for me. They are all looking for the Son.*

Aren't we all just looking for the Son, a bright ray to burn up our desperation from having too much or not enough?

Back at my kitchen table, our friend asked a difficult question that day in response to my story: "How do we tell the hungry of the world, 'Give us our daily bread'?"

His question turned my thoughts to the Lord's Prayer. Our family had memorized it around the very table at which we were sitting.

Pray then like this:

> "Our Father in heaven,
> hallowed be your name.
> Your kingdom come,
> your will be done,
>   on earth as it is in heaven.
> Give us this day our daily bread,
> and forgive us our debts,
>   as we also have forgiven our debtors.
> And lead us not into temptation,
>   but deliver us from evil." (Matt. 6:9–13 ESV)

My table has never lacked bread, and I have never known the kind of hunger our friend described. I have not experienced the desperation I saw on the faces of the mothers I met in Kenya. But in that moment in my kitchen with my discarded to-do list, I was desperate to hear his answer. I asked him to tell me how to reconcile both places, both peoples—those who do not have enough and those who have too much. "Traveling between the two places makes me thank God," he said. "Sometimes God asks us to be a bridge. And the challenge is to trust God because he is sovereign."

Sometimes God asks us to be a bridge—something that connects two places and peoples. I tucked his words away in my heart for when my feet are straddling two continents. But nonprofit leaders aren't the only bridges connecting the poor to the rich. Every believer is a bridge to an unbeliever. Our homes are the first places we should start building because we are bridges for our children to find God.

One of the most powerful things parents can give their kids is a view of the world. As adults we are all aware that there are millions of people in the world who don't have enough. Whether it's due to a lack of food, clean water, or money, they suffer because they don't have enough daily bread. If you're holding this book, you are likely privileged and don't fit into that category. The privileged have the holy command to share what they have been given.

In the process of writing this book I returned to Kenya with my family over spring break. We entered a home that was smaller than our master bathroom and squinted in the dark to find a place to sit. When our eyes adjusted to the light we cringed as bedbugs crawled all over us.

I couldn't believe seven people lived in this stifling, dark room. The heat wasn't as oppressive as the lack of hope. I slid my camera back into my bag because I knew there would be no pictures here. There weren't any smiling faces or laughing children. There was a heaviness in the air I can't explain.

The home belonged to the mother of one of the teen moms from the maternity home, and our staff in Kenya wanted us to understand why we needed a transition home for some of the girls and their children. And they needed us to know why providing jobs is so critical.

When we asked how we could pray for her, she shared about the difficult issues in her marriage and the abuse by her drunken husband. We held hands and prayed over her. It was hot and hard to shake the hopelessness that pervaded the room. Just as we were preparing to leave, her husband walked in the door—drunk.

And just like that, my little family was in the middle of a heated dispute in a dangerous slum with angry words being flung back and forth in Swahili. We sat back down. I held my little girl's hand and whispered a prayer for peace and safety as we sat there, unsure of what was being said. I won't lie—in that half hour I didn't feel brave at all and longed to return to my normal.

But as soon as I thought it I heard the words thunder in my heart: *This is their normal.*

I closed my eyes and silent tears slid down my cheeks. *My God, this is their normal. There isn't a fun week of spring break ahead. There isn't peace and provision. There isn't enough bread for the day. And as hard as this is to experience for an hour, this is their way of life.*

It's easy to get so absorbed in our own little worlds that we completely miss the way the rest of the world lives. And I can say this because it's what I did for a very long time. But I dare you, I beg you to hear this truth: *your normal isn't the world's normal, and the greatest deception is that you believe that it is.*

Your full pantry isn't normal for the rest of the world. Your cold fridge with your favorite drinks and closets with clothes and multiple pairs of shoes—this is not normal for 75 percent of the world. In economic terms the global North (United States, Canada, Western Europe, Australia, New Zealand)—with one quarter of the world's population—controls four-fifths of the income earned anywhere in the world. Inversely, the global South (every other country)—with three quarters of the world's population—has access to one-fifth of the world's income.[1]

In other words, a small percentage of us has access to most of the world's resources while a large percentage of the world doesn't have enough for one day. God uses people and builds bridges to connect the two worlds. But the life we are building is wasted if it doesn't take us somewhere that matters. It's tragic to build a bridge to nowhere. The only thing worse is leading our kids there.

The world and all its sparkling offerings give us temporary satisfaction. But we were created for the real thing. John Piper says, "If you don't feel strong desires for the manifestation of the glory of God, it is not because you have drunk deeply and are satisfied. It is because you have nibbled so long at the table of the world. Your soul is stuffed with small things, and there is no room for the great."[2]

It's tempting to think that those with more than enough always rescue those without enough. I have discovered a mutual rescue because I'm just as desperate to see the Son. So with a worldview that acknowledges some have less, others have more, and maybe, just maybe, God wants to use us as a bridge—we first need to answer the question, Why do we give?

51

I don't want to raise children who believe we are working our way to heaven, checking off an eternal list of good deeds to earn our way in and to somehow build a bridge high enough to get us there. No, our salvation is only by grace upon grace, mercy upon mercy.

I discovered how to teach this truth to my kids when a friend sent me a link to a devotion on the familiar parable found in Matthew 25:

> When he finally arrives, blazing in beauty and all his angels with him, the Son of Man will take his place on his glorious throne. Then all the nations will be arranged before him and he will sort the people out, much as a shepherd sorts out sheep and goats, putting sheep to his right and goats to his left.
>
> Then the King will say to those on his right, "Enter, you who are blessed by my Father! Take what's coming to you in this kingdom. It's been ready for you since the world's foundation. And here's why:
>
> > I was hungry and you fed me,
> > I was thirsty and you gave me a drink,
> > I was homeless and you gave me a room,
> > I was shivering and you gave me clothes,
> > I was sick and you stopped to visit,
> > I was in prison and you came to me."
>
> Then those "sheep" are going to say, "Master, what are you talking about? When did we ever see you hungry and feed you, thirsty and give you a drink? And when did we ever see you sick or in prison and come to you?" Then the King will say, "I'm telling the solemn truth: Whenever you did one of these things to someone overlooked or ignored, that was me—you did it to me."

Then he will turn to the "goats," the ones on his left, and say, "Get out, worthless goats! You're good for nothing but the fires of hell. And why? Because—

I was hungry and you gave me no meal,
I was thirsty and you gave me no drink,
I was homeless and you gave me no bed,
I was shivering and you gave me no clothes,
Sick and in prison, and you never visited."

Then those "goats" are going to say, "Master, what are you talking about? When did we ever see you hungry or thirsty or homeless or shivering or sick or in prison and didn't help?"

He will answer them, "I'm telling the solemn truth: Whenever you failed to do one of these things to someone who was being overlooked or ignored, that was me—you failed to do it to me."

Then those "goats" will be herded to their eternal doom, but the "sheep" to their eternal reward. (vv. 31–51)

The following excerpt from a devotion titled, "The Severe Mercy of a Pre-emptive Judgment" helped me to clearly understand the parable:

So is Jesus saying we are not, in fact, saved by grace alone through faith alone but by feeding the hungry, caring for the poor, clothing the naked, ministering to the sick and visiting those in prison? . . . How do we reconcile these un-minced words of Jesus that seem to say just the opposite?

Here's how I resolve it. . . . Nothing we can do, no matter how extraordinarily meritorious, can ever cancel our own unpayable debt and earn for us the grace of the forgiveness of Jesus Christ—NOTHING. I think Jesus is mercifully giving us the answers to the final exam. He's revealing to us what a person who is saved by grace alone through faith alone actually looks like in the midst of a fallen and mercilessly cruel world. The hallmark quality of a person who has received mercy is that they have become a person who shows mercy.

In this famous final judgment parable of the sheep and the goats, Jesus is offering us a severe mercy. He is giving us the gracious opportunity, right now, to examine ourselves preemptively according to the terms of the judgment before it actually happens. The question? Are we becoming the kind of people whose lives exude the evidence of having been saved by grace through faith?[3]

The words shook me to the core and reminded me of the *why* behind everything we do. This is *why* we should give. We should give to others because Jesus gave to us. We should extend mercy because we have received mercy. We don't give our time, money, and talent to show we are following Christ. We do it because we are Christ followers. This is Christianity.

So what does a generous family really look like? I can tell you that sometimes it looks like a family who is arguing at dinner and giving up on the devotional reading. Ask me how I know this.

I think it's dangerous to believe our family should be the holiest house on the block. If we buy into this lie, when we fail—*and we will fail*—succeeding will be even harder. I believe the mark of a family trying to bridge their lives to others is one that loves others well. It's easy to equate mission with action and traveling to the other side of the world, but mission is more than that. Loving others is a way of life; we don't have to squeeze one more event into our busy calendars to live a generous, missional life. It starts with opening our eyes to what's in front of us. We are surrounded by people in need and opportunities to love others: single moms on the soccer team, a friend with a new cancer diagnosis, an elderly neighbor recovering from surgery.

Following are four ways your family can live generously right where you are:

1. See the people around you. This requires more than just observing people; it means stopping to notice them.
2. Spot the needs in others' lives. When we take the time to get to know and develop relationships with the people around us, we'll easily recognize needs in their lives.
3. Scatter kindness. It's easy to care for and live in community with the people we've invested in. We can do this by going out of our way to take them a meal, offer childcare, and so on. This is how we love others well.
4. Start over with number one. When we make this a way of life, it changes everything. It becomes normal for our families to see the needs of others and to find a way to meet them.

I love taking Communion with my family. Our church offers it corporately every month, though it's also available weekly. There's just something very holy about breaking bread together and remembering the gift given. I usually cry, especially if my husband asks one of our kids to lead us in prayer during the reflective time when families circle together to take Communion. Or I cry when I pray. Okay, I cry no matter who prays.

Last Christmas we had a mess of a morning. There were tears and angry words, and it was a miracle we made it to the service at all. I hadn't shaken off the bad feelings the morning carried with it. When the congregation stood to take Communion I wanted to run. But when I tore off a piece of bread from the broken loaf I thought of my brokenness. Oh, I can make a mess of this life with my knack for attempting to control all the things that are out of my control. When I dipped that bit of bread into the red juice and it soaked up the liquid, I remembered that Jesus—the greatest gift—makes each day new and whole.

But Communion isn't just for Sundays or Christmas. It is a way of life—we are to be broken and shared. Ann Voskamp, in her book *The Broken Way*, describes how she and her family spent her birthday performing small acts of kindness and giving gifts around town. They left cookies on police cars and paid for coffee for a line of people at a coffee shop. She says:

> What we break and give comes back to us as a bit of communion. . . . When you walk into a diner across the street and tell the waitress you're paying for that family's dinner, it's a thing you don't forget, and it feels like an act of re-membering. The waitress laughs and you wink and leave before they're finished at the all-you-can-eat buffet. A diner and hungry people and the presence of Christ in you, reaching your unsure hand out, can taste like a sacrament.[4]

Ann explains the connection between Communion and thanksgiving earlier in the book:

> I hold the broken Last Supper in front of me, a Jesus with broken hands. What did Jesus do after He gave thanks? "And he took bread, gave thanks and broke it, and gave it to them." He took it and gave thanks—*eucharisteo*. Then he broke it and gave. How many times had I said it: "*Eucharisteo* precedes the miracle"? Thanksgiving precedes the miracle—the miracle of knowing all is enough. And how many times had I read it: "[Jesus] took the seven loaves and the fish, and when he had given thanks, he

broke them and gave them to the disciples, and they in turn to the people" (Matt. 16:36 NIV)? *Eucharisteo*—Jesus embracing and giving thanks for his not-enough—that preceded the miracle. But why hadn't I been awakened at the detonation of the revelation before? What was the actual miracle? The miracle happens in the breaking. Not-enough was given thanks for, and then the miracle happened: There was a breaking and a giving—into a kind of communion—into abundant filling within community. The miracle happens in the breaking.[5]

Acknowledging what we have and what the world lacks will break us. Becoming a bridge—a place to span the gulf in between us—will break us. It's in the breaking that we learn the true beauty of giving.

Ann is a dear friend, and when this book about brokenness was released, she sent me a copy along with a loaf of bread. I sat at my kitchen table and broke the loaf in two, then passed it to my son to tear off a piece. As we nibbled on the crusty loaf I thought of the holy man who had sat in the same spot and told me about the world that didn't have bread to eat. I swallowed my bite of bread and whispered a prayer for the hungry and desperate on both sides of the world, for those who have too much and those who don't have enough. "Give us this day, our daily bread. . . ."

Start
WORLD-CHANGING
CONVERSATIONS
with Your Kids

I asked my daughter Emerson to answer the following questions. I hope they lead to good conversations with your kids.

1. Have you ever been hungry? I mean, really, really hungry? What did you do about it? If I was really hungry and couldn't get any food I would go to my mom and ask her for some food. And if my mom didn't have food or for some reason ran out of food, I would try to find a way to help provide for my family. By then I would have my sister drive her car to the nearby grocery store. And if I did not have money I would ask my sister to get a job while I asked for money or told people I needed it for a family cause. But if we still had no money and no food I would try my best to think of a way to help my family. This makes me think about people around the world who don't have food. For a year my family and I ate rice and beans every Monday. We did this to experience what most of the world has to eat. It got old but it was a good reminder.

2. Why do you think some people have enough food and some people don't? I think some people don't have food because they don't have jobs or money to get food. Other people have plenty of food because they have jobs, money, and an education. In Kenya I was able to walk through the slums, and I saw trash everywhere and very small homes made of mud and scraps of metal. It made me feel like we have so much and they have hardly anything.

3. What do you think God wants us to do about it? I think God wants us to share food with others. But most of us are not very good at sharing. We keep everything to ourselves. When you have more than enough and you give something away, it makes you feel happy knowing you have made someone's day. Sometimes when you give even a little, other people will have food for weeks. For us it may be giving a little, but to them it feels like a lot. I think the best thing we can do is help them to get a job. We watched a documentary that showed giving only food or money doesn't help in the long run. We have to find a way to help that lasts.

4. Can you tell me why we take Communion at church? I think God wants us to take Communion at church so we can remember all that he has done for us. Jesus broke his body for us and shed his blood for us and died on the cross so that we could have our sins forgiven and have a relationship with him. When I take Communion I think about Jesus and how much he loves me. He was willing to die so that I could have life.

5. How do you think you can change the world? I think I can change the world by maybe giving some money to charities or by volunteering at a charity like Mercy House Global. I can change the world by purchasing fair-trade items and accessories at Mercy House. (I didn't tell her to say this, but I love that she did!)

Practice
GENEROSITY

- Read *The Giving Tree* by Shel Silverstein with your family and talk about the principles this fun book shares with the Bible.

- Host an Acts of Kindness day with friends and deliver baked goods to hospitals and police and fire stations.

- Get creative with a DIY bank project and make saving, giving, and spending banks. Set them in the kitchen or in a high traffic area of your home as a regular reminder. This is an easy way to teach kids about saving.

4

Is Our Extra a Blessing or a Test?

Christian maturity isn't marked by how much we know or what we can get, it's marked by how much we love and how much we give in light of how deeply we've been loved and how much we've been given.

Carey Nieuwhof

Church camp is our kids' favorite week of summer. They love the wild games, late nights, and community of friends. Summer camp was a month after my son's thirteenth birthday, and it was the first time all three of my kids would be gone at the same time, leaving the house to Terrell and me. You could say it was about to become our favorite week of summer too.

We lugged sleeping bags and duffle bags to the church early in the morning, hugged and kissed our kids enough times to embarrass them, and went out on a wonderful breakfast date at a restaurant they don't like. We sat on the same side of the corner booth, took a selfie, and told the world how much we missed our kids.

On the way home Terrell's phone rang. He put his hand over the phone and whispered, "It's the painter." I got excited. We had been on a waiting list for months to have the inside of our house painted by a contractor who gave us the best price. I had wanted to say good-bye to the builder-beige color for several years, and we had saved so that we could have it done professionally.

"Oh, you can come today? Really, right now? Hang on, let me ask my wife," Terrell said.

I shook my head no as I thought about our plans for the day, all the furniture and wall décor that would have to be moved, and how chaotic the whole week would be. But my husband said, "Honey, he had a cancellation and has an extra crew and can get started on the house right now, or we will have to wait another month. I think we should do it. The kids are gone. How bad can it be?"

Less than an hour later our walls were bare, the furniture was in the middle of the living room covered in plastic, and I was confirming paint swatches as a crew worked upstairs to prep the rooms. We had painters in and out of our home all week. I loved the subtle gray walls and decided the chaos was definitely worth it.

When we picked up our kids from camp, we couldn't wait to surprise them with their new room colors. They raced upstairs, and we heard squeals of delight. And then my son leaned over the balcony and said, "Hey, where's my wallet?"

Terrell and I looked at each other, and that's when I remembered Jon-Avery had his Christmas, birthday, and lawn-mowing money in his wallet—more than three hundred dollars—waiting to be deposited once he got home. I remembered seeing his bulging wallet on his desk, but I didn't think to put it away when the work crew arrived at the house. We went upstairs to help him find it, searched the entire house, and made phone calls. It was gone, along with his pocketknife. Even all these years later, that leather wallet has never shown up.

We could only assume it had been stolen, and we felt terrible about it. We promised to help replace the money, but Jon-Avery's response surprised me: "Mom, it's okay. I had more than I needed, and I wasn't really saving for anything. Maybe the person who took it needed it more than I did."

I looked at him as if he were crazy because I know if my life savings had disappeared I wouldn't have extended as much grace. I hugged him and chewed on his words for days. I asked God to help me hold what I own more loosely—like my son.

Jesus tells two stories about two people and their money that offer a stark contrast. In Mark we read about the poor widow who gave her two small coins, equivalent to a penny, and we warm to Jesus's praise: "She, out of her poverty, put in everything" (12:44 NIV). I've always wondered about this woman tossing her gift into the offering plate, surrounded by religious people who gave much more. Did she give everything she had because she knew it would be returned or because of the joy she felt when she gave or maybe both?

There are many lessons we can take away from this story. Jesus sees things differently than the world does since he noted her small offering rather than the others' large ones; Jesus doesn't do math the way we do. He doesn't want a little, he wants it all. It's not about the fact that we give; anyone can give. But does it cost us something? For the rich, their offerings cost them nothing. For the widow, her offering cost her everything. Jesus praised her because she gave it all. Her offering cost her significantly more than the offering given by the rich.

Jesus wants us to give what we have. It's not about the size of the gift; it's the size of our heart that matters. Let's face it, in our culture of bigger is better, sometimes it feels like our little yes isn't enough. I love these words from Mahatma Gandhi, "Whatever you do will be insignificant, but it is very important that you do it."[1]

In contrast, Jesus introduces us to a rich young ruler who wasn't willing to give up everything he had for a greater treasure. When he asked Jesus about how to receive eternal life, he wasn't willing to do what Jesus asked of him: "Sell your possessions and give to the poor, and you will have treasure in heaven. Then come, follow me" (Matt. 19:21 NIV).

The passage goes on to say:

> "Truly I tell you, it is hard for someone who is rich to enter the kingdom of heaven. Again I tell you, it is easier for a camel to go through the eye of a needle than for someone who is rich to enter the kingdom of God."
>
> When the disciples heard this, they were greatly astonished and asked, "Who then can be saved?"
>
> Jesus looked at them and said, "With man this is impossible, but with God all things are possible." (vv. 23–26 NIV)

I have always been a little afraid of this story; I worried that God might ask me to do the same thing. Would I be willing to give all I have if he asked me to?

What might God ask us to give up? God wants us to give him what we love the most because our love of _____ (fill in the blank) will keep us from God. This was an influential man, maybe even a prince, who had everything money could buy. But when Jesus asked him to give up what he loved the most—his money and possessions—he walked away sad and empty because he just couldn't do it. Jesus's command revealed an ugly truth: the young man loved something of the world more than he loved Jesus. Money was his idol.

Jesus asked him to give up what he treasured most, knowing that money and possessions were the young ruler's god. Randy Alcorn states it this way: "Jesus knew the rich young ruler wouldn't serve God unless he dethroned his money idol. But the seeker considered the price too great. Sadly, he walked away from real treasures."[2]

When we dig deeply into God's Word we discover this truth to share with our children: how we live impacts how we give.

The rich young ruler mistook the temporary satisfaction of his riches for something that would last and passed up eternity with God. This choice directly impacted how he lived.

My daughter Emerson has always had a sweet tooth. She used to bang the tray of her high chair for pureed fruits and pucker her lips at everything else offered. Her eyes light up at slices of cake and pink donuts and cheesecake. Cupcakes may be her love language. Don't even get me started on how often she asks for candy. She is a picky eater, and dinner is always a battle; of course, she's always hungry for dessert. Maybe this sounds familiar. We joke about her insatiable appetite for sugar and constantly remind her to fill up on good food first. The other day she had a lightbulb moment, "Mom, when I eat something sweet, it tastes so good, but I'm usually still hungry afterward."

Her epiphany made me think about raising our kids in a culture on a constant quest for satisfaction. I've watched my kids fill up on empty things—from social media cravings to the trendy, must-have fashion fads to the latest technology upgrades. And one thing is certain: even if or when they get what they want, there's always something next or better around the corner tempting them.

In our culture no matter how much we get we always want more because we are really good at filling up our time and our lives with things that do not satisfy. Although these things may not all be bad, they leave us feeling empty instead of full. As a matter of fact, it's reported that after reading other people's statuses on Facebook we're more likely to feel down and depressed and generally worse about ourselves than before we read them.[3] I know I've experienced this.

We are raising a tween and two teens in our house, and I have watched them go from one thing to another in their quest to be satisfied—from sports to musical instruments to hairstyles. I realize this is part of growing up, but it has been amazing watching my older two (especially in the last six or so months) discover deep, abiding satisfaction in their relationship with Christ. They are discovering truths that will carry them through whatever life brings their way. Filling their hearts and minds with the things of God will satisfy their hunger in a way that the world cannot. They will not only feel better but will also be full.

It's tough being a parent. Our kids are looking to us to lead them. Yet it's so easy to satisfy our hunger for the eternal with the temporary; it's easy to get offtrack. When we embrace eternal truths for ourselves, we can lead our kids into God's definition of satisfaction. I was middle-aged before I got there (and some days I still need a big reminder), so give yourself a break and bookmark the following four conversations to have with your kids.

1. *We are eternal beings.* This life isn't the end. Despite our striving and obtaining, we all leave this world with the same thing—nothing. We are created for eternity. The things of this world that are fun and feel good are temporary. They will not last. Kids don't always have the perspective of hindsight, so everything here and now feels like forever. They need us to gently remind them that the things of this world will never satisfy the hunger with which we are born.

2. *We can't hold on and let go at the same time.* Ask your kids to hold on to both your hands while also gripping the handlebars of their bikes. It's impossible. We have to let go of one or the other. Talk about the story of the rich young ruler with them. He was a good guy; he had done good things. But in the end he held on to the things that didn't matter. Scripture tells us, "He was holding on tight to a lot of things, and he couldn't bear to let go" (Matt. 19:22). We have to teach our kids we can't hold on to Jesus until we let go of this world.

3. *We were created to do something that matters.* As Christians, if our life goal is happiness we are missing the point of life. We aren't here so we can have it all or do it all. If that's our aim we will live dissatisfied lives. We are here to glorify God with our lives. God wants to know that we love him more than anything else. When we live out our purposes we find deep satisfaction, and we discover that our cravings for something real and sweet are satisfied as well. Ask your child what they love doing and look for ways to encourage them to do it for Jesus.

4. *Our heart will lead us to our treasure.* Jesus said, "Where your treasure is, there your heart will be also" (Matt. 6:21 NIV). This is a hard saying, but we cannot deny the truth of it. Where we give our time, money, passion, and energy is where we are

investing our hearts and lives. If we made a list of the things we're investing in or put them in a pie chart, what would it reveal?

Jesus gives us clear, simple instructions regarding our treasures:

> Do not store up for yourselves treasures on earth, where moths and vermin destroy, and where thieves break in and steal. But store up for yourselves treasures in heaven, where moths and vermin do not destroy, and where thieves do not break in and steal. For where your treasure is, there your heart will be also. (vv. 19–21 NIV)

And so this begs the question, What do we treasure?

When Jon-Avery was in preschool he had a treasure box. At first it wasn't an actual box; it was his pockets. He loved stuffing things in his pockets, and I learned the hard way that lizards and frogs drown in the washing machine. From small reptiles he moved on to every kind of screw, nut, bolt, watch part, battery, and metal wire he discovered around the house or in the garage. As he referred to his collection as treasures, we gave him a wooden treasure box to keep his prizes in. Since that time we've always said Jon-Avery will probably grow up to be an engineer. For years, he took apart anything that was broken to see how it worked—clocks, toys, and once a laptop keyboard. He tucked the tiny parts away in his box. One time I caught him unscrewing a doorknob so he could store the screws. When he visited his grandparents' farm in Oklahoma, his grandpa took him to his shop where he worked on farm equipment and gave Jon-Avery treasures for his box. Everyone knew what he treasured.

Sometimes we find it difficult to define what we treasure. We can't open a box and see them. But when God looks in our hearts they are evident. In his book *Money, Possessions, and Eternity*, Randy Alcorn asks this question: What is our treasure? A. W. Tozer suggests we may discover the answer by responding to four basic questions:

1. What do we value most?
2. What would we most hate to lose?
3. What do our thoughts turn to most frequently when we are free to think of what we will?
4. What affords us the greatest pleasure?[4]

Obviously, Jesus is the greatest treasure. But would our lives reveal this truth? Would how we live and what we give make it obvious to others that he is our treasure?

In 2010 when I traveled to Kenya with Compassion International on a blogging trip (I write about it in *Rhinestone Jesus: Saying Yes to God When Sparkly Safe Faith Is No Longer Enough*), I discovered my treasure wasn't Jesus, and it broke me. I identified with Wess Stafford's confession: "I avoided coming to visit the poor . . . for a long time. I was afraid my heart would be broken by their condition. Instead, today, I found my heart broken by my condition."[5]

I've spent the time since seeking my satisfaction in Jesus. Don't get me wrong. I was a good person, a faithful wife, an intentional mother, and a regular churchgoer, but I was satisfying myself with treasures that would not last. I was full of things that left me feeling empty. I was pious and judged those who weren't like me, and I was wrecked when I discovered just how poor I really was. *I* was the rich young ruler. I was the Christian that David Platt referred to in his book *Radical*:

So what is the difference between someone who willfully indulges in sexual pleasures while ignoring the Bible on moral purity and someone who willfully indulges in the selfish pursuit of more and more material possessions while ignoring the Bible on caring for the poor? The difference is that one involves a social taboo in the church and the other involves the social norm in the church.[6]

I had always thought that what I had been given was a blessing for me to keep rather than a gift for me to share with others. But hoarding didn't satisfy me like I thought it would. Instead it robbed me of joy. And worse, I was teaching my children the same thing by living a poor example in front of them.

When we are blessed with money or possessions—or robbed of them—is it a blessing or a test? In *The Treasure Principle*, a tiny book on giving that packs a powerful punch, Alcorn states:

God comes right out and tells us why He gives us more money than we need. It's not so we can find more ways to spend it. It's not so we can indulge ourselves and spoil our children. It's not so we can insulate ourselves from needing God's provision.

It's so we can *give*—generously.

When God provides more money, we often think, *This is a blessing*. Well, yes, but it would be just as scriptural to think, *This is a test*.[7]

I have failed this test many times. I spent a big chunk of my life seeing extra provision as a blessing for me and my family so that we could have more. But the more I got, the emptier I felt. When we started sharing what we'd been given, we discovered true joy: it is better to give than to receive.

I think Platt sums it up best:

[At the end of our lives] we will not wish we had made more money, acquired more stuff, lived more comfortably, taken more vacations, watched more television, pursued greater retirement, or been more successful in the eyes of this world. Instead, we will wish we had given more of ourselves to living for the day when every nation, tribe, people, and language will bow around the throne and sing the praises of the Savior who delights in radical obedience and the God who deserves eternal worship.[8]

Start WORLD-CHANGING CONVERSATIONS *with Your Kids*

I asked my son, Jon-Avery, to answer the following questions. I hope they lead to good conversations with your kids.

1. What do you value most? Six months ago I think the brutally honest truth would have been archery. Every day rushing through school so I could shoot for hours on end so I could improve and get better. It was a pursuit that consumed me. It was my passion, but it had evolved into a selfish obsession; you could say it had become my god. Going to Africa my sixth time was incredibly more sobering than I could have imagined. I went on the trip thinking I was a veteran, thinking that nothing I saw could have any more gravity than it had in the past. I came back more impacted than I had ever been before.

On the eve of my trip I went to the tournament I had been obsessively training for in the previous six months. I shot the worst I had ever shot in my life and ranked lower than I thought possible. I had never thought of myself as very prideful. But coming in last place in front of all my fellow competitors, my family, and my new coach revealed to me how prideful and arrogant I was and how meaningless my life had become.

Contrasting my selfish obsession to the men and women who were changing lives every day, going into the pit of hell and rescuing innocent girls from the depths of poverty—girls I had come to love like family—opened up my eyes to my life. I did not shoot again until a week after I returned home. Taking that month off was so good for me. I saw that archery had become my world and my god. Realizing that the sense of purpose I thought I found in archery had become distorted and wrong was crushing. Reading this chapter, I cannot help but apply the words to my own life. What if I was not given archery just so that I could compete and do well in the sport? What if the whole journey I have been on—being impacted and mentored by my coach, going through struggle after struggle with my shooting, facing injury and grief—has been to enable me to pour into other people through archery? Maybe all this happened to me so I would see this, so I would shoot with a new purpose and be intentional with people, so I would look for every opportunity to impact and influence those I meet. It is a very challenging thing to contemplate, but doing so has given me new purpose in my shooting and in my life. It has been very humbling for me to come to this conclusion. I have wrestled with it for a long while. But after all is said and done, I will look back at my life to see what I have done with it. At this stage in my life I know that repurposing my passion and making it pure in Jesus is what I am supposed to do.

2. **What do your thoughts turn to most frequently when you are free to think of what you will?** In our fast-paced culture, it can be so easy to be swept away with the constant stimulants and activities. We have come up with endless ways to entertain ourselves and keep ourselves busy. When I take time to escape this

nonstop activity, my thoughts drift to my purpose. I have thought long and hard about it and beyond Jesus I can think of no other meaning to life. I cannot come up with a purpose that will give me enough meaning to keep living. When my mind drifts to that place, it motivates me to keep my thoughts centered there. I find that when I go through the day thinking about how I can live my life with purpose, I see instances and opportunities to live out my faith. If I start my day there, then whenever I am tempted, I am able to resist by thinking of how I am living out my purpose. Every time I am confronted with an opportunity to share my faith or put it on display I am strengthened and empowered by the purpose motivating me.

3. What affords you the greatest pleasure? I think that the greatest pleasure I have ever experienced in my life is the joy of feeling God's presence. I can't explain it, but in those moments all my fear is gone—all my apprehension and anxiety, all my worry for the day. When I am worshiping Jesus, I experience this. I can let go of everything and put it on the cross. One thing that has been liberating for me is how wide worship is. It is not constrained to Sunday morning hymns and not elevated to something unreachable. Worshiping God can be through prayer, praises, sharing the gospel, or meeting the needs you see in Jesus's name. You can express your thankfulness however you want, so long as it's meaningful and heartfelt. Experiencing worship is truly something else, and it is by far the best thing that can be felt on this earth.

Practice
GENEROSITY

- Be a secret Santa for a single parent. Shop for age-appropriate toys, deliver wrapped packages in the dark, ring the doorbell, and pull around the corner to watch the delight.

- Host houseguests and ask your kids to give up their rooms.

5

Giving Our Homes a Generosity Overhaul

> Our greatest fear should not be of failure but of
> succeeding at things in life that don't really matter.
>
> Frances Chan

I will never forget the day my teenager gave me a generosity overhaul.

As often as we can afford to, we take our kids with us to Kenya to visit our maternity and transition homes, artisan groups, and the graduates we support through Mercy House. It's an amazing opportunity, and my kids probably have no idea how lucky they are to see the world. But it's not a vacation, although we typically use all the vacation money we can save. It's actually a grueling trip with very little sleep, heavy traffic, a hectic schedule, and a lot of poverty and suffering for our hearts to take in. It's a perspective overload that is often overwhelming.

But we realized early on that our choice to change the world significantly changed our kids' worlds too. So we made the decision to include them as often as we could.

Several years ago we discovered it didn't cost any more money to stay a night or two in the city of our layover between continents. We sat down as a family and counted up the years the five of us had left together before my oldest went off to college and made a bucket list. It was one of the best decisions we ever made, and it has felt like a gift we've received in the middle of our giving. In the last three family trips over the past five years on our way home from Kenya, we've quickly explored Paris, Amsterdam, and Rome in a jet-lagged haze.

It has been a great way to make family memories and see the world, and it has made the harsh reality of reentering our culture of excess a little easier. It has also been the hotbed of some of our worst fights, such as the time we got on the wrong train and one of our kids nearly didn't make it off, or the time we sat in the Paris airport with maps we couldn't read and cried for an hour because we didn't know how to get to the cheap hotel I'd booked on Expedia. Fun times! Exhaustion and foreign countries are a dangerous combination.

Madison has struggled with motion sickness for most of her life, and it has gotten worse as she has gotten older. Traveling is hard on her body. But it doesn't stop her because she loves exploring new places. I've written about some of my anxiety issues, and she has inspired me to face them as I've watched her struggle with being sick or scared on just about every continent. When she was fourteen years old we gave her an old tour book we'd found at Goodwill and asked her to plan our visit for the two days we would be in the Netherlands. She was excited about visiting Amsterdam and fell in love with the city she had researched. We visited Anne Frank's tiny apartment in a holy hush, walked the iconic canals, ate pancakes the size of our heads, and rode a bus to the busy shopping district during the World Cup. It was a stark comparison to the slums we had visited in Kenya and the difficult stories we carried home with us. At the same time it was good for our family because life is a balance. As much as we want to be givers, it's healthy to be receivers too. Taking breaks, having fun, and making family memories make the giving even sweeter.

Madison loves the arts and fashion and asked if we could go into one of the towering stores in the Amsterdam city center. She tried on scarves and clothes and left excited about the purchase of a new skirt from Europe! As we walked out of the store I struggled to fit all I had seen the day before in Kenya with the excess I was surrounded by in Europe. The struggle isn't new for me, and I'm always trying to find a balance and not lean too far to one side or the other. I was processing this when Madison leaned over, swinging her bag with her latest fashion find, and said, "Mom, I think I know what I want to be when I grow up."

In fairness to Madison, she had no idea what I was struggling with. She was a kid who had always dreamed of shopping in Europe, and in that moment her dream had come true. I've learned in our international travels how much better my kids compartmentalize and process the stark differences they see between home and Kenya. They take things in stride and accept them for what they are often better than I do. Typically, I worry about how they will handle the poverty and suffering they are exposed to, but often they teach me how to handle these things by handling them so well themselves. Then sometimes, weeks or months later, I'm able to help them unravel and process hard questions and the aftermath of what they've witnessed.

"What, honey?" I asked with expectation. I won't lie; I held my breath because I thought her proclamation would be huge—world changing. I was raising world changers, after all. "Mom, I think I want to be a makeup artist."

I stopped on the ancient cobbled path and turned and looked at her to see if she was serious. "Really?" I said in a tone that literally snuffed the light right out of her eyes. And then I said, "We just left the poor in Kenya. I was hoping you would say something more . . . significant."

Madison's face fell in a way I had never seen before, and she turned and walked away from me. I was left following behind.

I will never, ever forget what it feels like to crush your child's dreams. It's a feeling I wish I didn't know.

I chased her down that cobbled path, but I couldn't erase the damage my careless words had caused. I didn't realize that my statement would be the start of a difficult journey for Madison—an unspoken pressure to do something significant, something big, something befitting a world changer with her life and to set aside her gifts and her dreams and conform to a mold that I had unintentionally created in ignorance.

More than a year later our family was having another difficult discussion about what generosity had cost our family. My teens were trying to decide how to complete high school. Giving away your time and resources isn't free, and living different from the world makes you feel different from the world you live in. They decided to transition out of public high school and for the first time become homeschoolers. Madison spoke up, "I just don't know what I want to do after high school. I don't know what to study in college. What if it's not significant? What if I don't want to lead a nonprofit some day?"

I responded, "What? Honey, where is this coming from? You can be and do whatever you want." And in a sudden flashback that conversation in Amsterdam came back to me and nearly knocked me over. I could see that she still believed the lie I had spoken into her tender heart. I grabbed her arms and pulled her close. She was reluctant. "I don't care what you do as long as you do it for Jesus. Listen closely to me. Do that thing you can't not do. Do what you were created for and offer it to God, and you will change the world. Be a makeup artist for Jesus because you will reach people I could never reach. You can change the world in a way I can't."

She looked at me as if I were crazy. "A makeup artist?" I realized she didn't remember the details of our conversation in Amsterdam, and I was grateful for small mercies. But she did remember feeling the pressure to do something significant, and I will never forget the lesson she taught me about my lack of generosity.

Madison reminded me that Jesus wants what we have. He doesn't want us to give what someone else has or do something someone else does. Raising world changers starts by loving our kids for who they are and by encouraging them to follow their passions. When we do this, we teach them there is a God-given purpose behind their talent or passion and we encourage them to pursue what they love. God gives us gifts to be given away. I heard this quote from Martin Luther King Jr. in church one Sunday and quickly wrote it down: "If a man is called to be a street sweeper, he should sweep streets even as Michelangelo painted, or Beethoven composed music, or Shakespeare wrote poetry. He should sweep streets so well that all the hosts of

81

heaven and earth will pause to say, 'Here lived a great street sweeper who did his job well.'"[1] God makes us unique so we can change the world in our unique way. This is the heart of generosity.

When I was honest with myself, I discovered four reasons I wasn't generous in my response to Madison that day. I believe these reasons also plague our culture and even cause the church to lean toward a posture of clenching what we hold tightly instead of opening our hands freely.

1. *Selfishness.* We naturally and even automatically think of ourselves first. How will this affect me? What will this mean for me? When I peeled back the layers of my response to Madison's statement I saw pride and selfishness, and it was ugly. No one has to teach us to be selfish, but we do have to train ourselves to be selfless.

2. *Ignorance.* We are not generous because we don't know or choose not to know how other people feel or live. Or we refuse to acknowledge that what we have is more than enough. Selfishness often blinds us so that we only see ourselves and are ignorant of other people's situations. Of course, enlightenment happens when we choose to see the light.

3. *Fear.* Fear is one of the biggest foes of generosity. We are afraid of the unknown, and we simply don't trust that God has our and our child's best interest in mind. We are also afraid of what we can't control (see me waving my hand in the air). So we clamp down on what we can control—our money, time, and kids.

4. *Lack of trust.* Lack of trust goes hand in hand with fear. We believe we know what is best for our lives and our family's lives. We don't give because we don't trust that God will continue to provide what we need. I recently heard a Bible teacher

claim that the word *trust* is a much better translation of the word *faith* in the Bible because it denotes action. The next time you read a passage with the word *faith* in it, try substituting the word *trust* and see how the revision changes the way you look at God's Word.

I love the way The Message translates James 2:14–18. The section is subtitled "Faith in Action." Or trust in action?

> Dear friends, do you think you'll get anywhere in this if you learn all the right words but never do anything? Does merely talking about faith [trust] indicate that a person really has it? For instance, you come upon an old friend dressed in rags and half-starved and say, "Good morning, friend! Be clothed in Christ! Be filled with the Holy Spirit!" and walk off without providing so much as a coat or a cup of soup—where does that get you? Isn't it obvious that God-talk without God-acts is outrageous nonsense?
>
> I can already hear one of you agreeing by saying, "Sounds good. You take care of the faith [trust] department, I'll handle the works department."
>
> Not so fast. You can no more show me your works apart from your faith [trust] than I can show you my faith [trust] apart from my works. Faith [trust] and works, works and faith [trust], fit together hand in glove.

Givers do something. They don't just talk; they act. When I think of generous people, I don't always think of those who are generous financially. I think of people like Shannon, for example. For years she cut and colored my hair in the bathroom in her house. She chose a home salon to keep her costs down and offered her services at a discount and by donation so people like me who couldn't afford hundreds of dollars at salons could hide their gray in dignity. But she didn't just do my hair around my schedule; she usually fed me too. Watching Shannon in the kitchen was like watching an artist paint a canvas. She loved to bake and prepared amazing meals. One week she even sent me home with not only great hair but also a complete homemade meal for my family after hearing I'd had a stressful day. She showed up more than once at Mercy House and shared delicious homemade cookies. Shannon gave away what she'd been given. She understood her gifts and shared them with others.

I don't know if Martin Luther King Jr. ever got to stand in a reverent hush while craning his neck to view the ceiling of the Sistine Chapel that Michelangelo spent years painting, but I have with my husband and kids. I'm so grateful that God is working on our kids despite our mistakes as parents. Sometimes he offers us a foreshadowing of who they are becoming, and we see a masterpiece in the making.

Last year God gave me a brief look into Madison's heart, and it is a stunning treasure.

"Mom, are you awake?"

Uh-huh.

It was 3:00 a.m. and Madison, my brand-new seventeen-year-old at the time, was lying next to me in a double bed in a small New York City hotel room. We had spent the day meeting fair-trade artisan groups I work with at Mercy House.

I had decided to take an impromptu trip to the Big Apple to visit the Handmade Global Market and see if it might be a good place for our nonprofit to wholesale our fair-trade product in the future as a way to provide more jobs for the impoverished women we empower. At the last minute I decided to bring Madison with me.

She has style, has her finger on the pulse of market trends, and is wildly artistic, and I knew this trip would impact her—not just because it was New York City, a place she'd always wanted to visit, but also because of where she was in life.

"Mom, thank you for bringing me with you," she whispered into the dark hotel room.

"You're welcome, honey. I'm glad you're here."

Heavy silence. She wasn't done.

"Mom?"

I waited.

"I just want you to know that I love you. And, um, I want to say thank you for starting Mercy House. Because it has changed our lives."

I swallowed the lump in my throat and let her continue.

"I know it's hard and you worry about the impact Mercy House has had on us kids. A few years ago I felt lost and then angry, and I wondered where God was. But, Mom? I'm proud to be your daughter, and I love where God has taken us."

Wet tears slipped down my cheeks and soaked my pillowcase. She wasn't done. We talked for more than an hour in the dark. We shared sweet words that felt holy and wholly needed.

"Honey, parenting is so hard. When it's all said and done, I just want to lead you to Jesus," I whispered, afraid to say more lest the dam break.

"You have, Mom."

I silently thanked God for the conversation. It didn't change anything, but it changed everything. The next day we were still the same mother-daughter duo arguing over where to eat, but our relationship had deepened and we both knew it. I could see the new respect in my daughter's face as she watched me interact with nonprofit leaders and answer questions about fair-trade product.

I have wondered where this wild obedience would take me. I have also worried it had taken my kids to a place of resentment and regret, and some days it has, because shifting and shaping our lives to orbit around Jesus is often difficult and painful. My yes to God has taken me away from my family, but it's given my kids a chance to lean on Jesus when they can't lean on me. It's required my kids to give up their bedrooms and beds on occasion, but it's given them an opportunity to learn hospitality. It's cost us some comforts, but it's given us a chance to offer comfort.

My biggest fear isn't that my choices, this path, will make the way tougher for my kids because I know that they have. My biggest fear is that they might not go where I've been too afraid to lead them. My dreams and detours and dead ends influence my children's stories. If I'm too afraid to step into the unknown or to live a generous life, they may be too.

Our kids don't need our protection in the unknown half as much as they need to see us persevere in the known. Our kids don't need our provision nearly as much as they need us to live with purpose. So as you read these words, hear my heart and do what God is asking you to do. Don't *not* do it because it will affect your kids. Maybe if they see you focusing less on them and more on others, it will impact them to do the same. Maybe interrupting your life will interrupt theirs. And maybe it will be good.

I turned over, sleep was close, and I brushed my daughter's hair away from her face. She yawned and said sleepily, "Mom, thanks for bringing me with you." We both knew she wasn't talking about New York.

Giving changes our home because it takes us on a beautiful journey of discovery. When we give, it impacts others. It turns us from selfish people into sacrificial ones. Generosity is risky, but great risk offers great rewards.

Raising world changers starts with letting them be who God created them to be. Sometimes we can help them discover just who they are by leaving our comfort zones. Getting out of our cultural bubble of safety and security has taught us many valuable lessons in generosity. But you don't have to leave the country to learn them. Serving refugees or the homeless in the heart of your city, visiting a nursing home, volunteering at a women's shelter, fostering kids, opening your life to people who are different from you, or doing something that risks your comfort will set your family up in the classroom of life.

Following are eleven lessons we've learned about generosity:

1. *When we leave what we know, we discover what we don't know.* The way we live isn't the way the world lives. Stepping out of what we know is eye opening.

2. *Discomfort is a great way to appreciate comfort.* I can't think of a better way to create an environment of gratitude than by being temporarily uncomfortable.

3. *Fear will paralyze us if we let it. Trust will thrust us into adventure.* Risk can be scary, but if we only do what we've always done we are limiting ourselves. With wisdom and trust in God, we can live an adventure.

4. *Bad things can happen in the middle of our comfort zones too. We can't let the fear of the unknown stop us from living.* The safest place for our family is wherever Jesus leads us. We aren't called to safety, and what's completely safe these days anyway?

5. *We really don't have as much control as we think we do.* Travel of any kind reminds us how little control we really have. It's also true of life and especially parenting. We

can't control everything or everyone; letting go is a great way to grow.

6. *Our strengths and weaknesses are revealed in the unknown.* I discovered one of my kids is a natural-born tour guide. She loves leading our family to unknown places. We've also discovered a whole list of weaknesses (such as don't give Mom the map) about each other.

7. *We need each other a little more when we are uncomfortable.* Nothing creates a family team spirit like the unknown. We realize we aren't quite as tough or as independent when we are unsure, but it's okay because we have each other and we discover together.

8. *We change our perspective.* I'm a huge fan of perspective. We need to shake things up to become more grateful for what we have. Nothing gives us a new perspective more than seeing how other people live.

9. *We create memories that will outlast anything we can buy.* By far our best memories have been made outside of our comfort zone. And hopefully we are teaching our kids that people and places are more important than stuff.

10. *We become more compassionate.* When we break out of our bubble, we open our eyes to people around us. It becomes the fertile ground in which compassion is born and grows.

11. *We see God more clearly.* Risk positions us to reach out to God—to ask for help, to pray for peace, and to see the world a little better and God a little bigger.

Start
WORLD-CHANGING
CONVERSATIONS
with Your Kids

I asked my daughter Madison to answer the following questions. I hope they lead to good conversations with your kids.

1. What have you learned about generosity? I have learned a lot about generosity and the impact it can have on your life through Mercy House, but one of the most significant things I've learned is that generosity makes you a genuinely happier and healthier person. I honestly think I am at my happiest when I am being generous because I'm not focusing on me or my problems or things that don't matter; I'm focusing on others. When we focus on others and turn our attention away from ourselves, I think God really uses that to work in our hearts and point us back to him. We learn that there are more important things in life, and we get to see the way that we can impact others. There's nothing like the feeling that gives.

2. How can parents encourage kids to give? I think parents can encourage kids to give by leading by example. Some of my earliest memories of giving and generosity were of my parents tithing and showing us that it is important to give back and share what we have. I remember at the young age of six or seven being given a dollar or two to give as an offering and then being instructed to set aside some of my own money to give my own offering. These memories and practices shaped my view of giving and generosity because I had parents who understood the value and importance of giving. I have watched my parents selflessly give over and over again, and their giving encourages me to do the same. When I see the way it affects them and how good it makes them feel, I want to do the same.

3. Why do you think kids don't give? I think kids and people in general don't give because of our selfish and sinful human nature. Also, we live in a society and world that are extremely inwardly focused and selfish; society tells us that our happiness and our lives are the most important things in the world. Many people are sheltered and are ignorant of the way the majority of the world lives, and it is so easy to find yourself in a selfish bubble separated from the rest of the world. I think we need God and his Word to help us understand and acknowledge and practice giving because he is the greatest example of what giving means.

4. What would you tell parents who are reading this who are worried or discouraged about the path their kids are on? I remember something my youth pastor told me about those who are lost and far from Christ, and it really encouraged me. He said that as Christians it's our job to plant seeds in people. However, we're not the ones responsible for creating a mature plant; that's God's job. All we can do as Christians is plant seeds in the hearts of those around us. It's not our job to transform lives or make true changes because only God can do that. However, we can shine light on those seeds, water them, and encourage them to grow. I think that parents who are discouraged about the path their kids are on should just keep planting seeds and nurturing and watering those seeds because that's what God calls us to do. It's important to remember our role and to also understand and remind ourselves that it's not our job to transform others; we are simply the sowers of seeds. God has a plan for each and every one of us, and that plan usually doesn't look anything like we think it will. I think it's important for us to rely on God and to truly trust him, no matter where we are right now, knowing that he has a good plan for each and every one of us.

Practice
GENEROSITY

- Give your time away. Take a class and become respite caregivers for foster-care families in your town.

- Let your kids fail. It may sound harsh, but when they fail we are giving them an opportunity to overcome. Overcoming makes them more compassionate, and they see themselves and others differently from this perspective.

- Pay it forward in a drive-through.

6

The High Cost of Giving Our Lives Away

> I ask you to do one thing: do not tire of giving, but do not give your leftovers. Give until it hurts, until you feel the pain.
>
> Mother Teresa

I never meant to be the elementary room mom for all three of my kids. It just sort of happened by default. When Madison was in kindergarten I was like most first-time school mothers, eager to help and be involved in my child's education. We hit the kindergarten jackpot by accident with Mrs. Davis. She had been teaching five-year-olds for twenty years, and her classroom theme was, "You get what you get and you don't throw a fit." She was easy to love, and I loved being her room mom as much as Madison loved her first year of school. Two years later, when Jon-Avery started school and we landed in Mrs. Davis's class again, I had the opportunity to put into practice all she'd taught me two years before.

We started Mercy House when Madison was in fourth grade, Jon-Avery was in second, and Emerson was just three years old. That yes to God started a ripple effect of one life change after another for our family, and we decided to move to a nearby town where we could live on less and grow roots for our nonprofit. By the time Emerson started school I was a work-from-home mom, and I didn't really have time to be a room mom. But I hadn't quite learned to conquer mom guilt, and when no one else volunteered I reluctantly agreed to fill in. I made sure everyone knew that this was my last year. And it was, until I got a phone call from Emerson's first-grade teacher in the middle of the day. After she assured me Emerson was fine, she asked if I would please be the first-grade room mom. I didn't tell her I had just started writing my memoir, *Rhinestone Jesus*, and the December 1 deadline loomed. So I was just as surprised as you might be that I hung up the phone as room mom once again. I suspected I might have a problem saying no.

But I like to think it was providential because this was the year God taught me two truths that have shaped every day since. First, obedience is better than sacrifice, and second, we are where we are for a reason. I'll never forget the day Emerson came home from school just before Thanksgiving break and casually said during dinner, "Mom, we have a new girl, Avery, in our class, and she wears paper beads like our girls make in Kenya."

My head snapped up from my plate of tacos. I immediately began interrogating my six-year-old. "Where did she get paper beads?" Paper-bead jewelry was just starting to get popular but not with first graders, so I knew this was odd.

"Ethiopia. She lived there," she said between bites.

"Are you sure she lived in Ethiopia? Did you tell her you're going back to Kenya for Thanksgiving break, and you have paper beads too?" I fired away at her.

Emerson looked at me from across the table as if I had totally lost it. And considering the average family dinner conversation, she was probably right. But it just seemed more than a coincidence. Over the next few days I questioned her after school, probing for more information. I learned that the new family had adopted two boys from Ethiopia before they moved, and they were currently living with extended family down the street from us.

We went on that trip to Kenya to work at the maternity homes and took our kids out of school a few extra days to explore Paris on our layover on the way home. On that trip I wrote the epilogue to *Rhinestone Jesus* and submitted it a week later. "There, I'm done!" I said to Terrell as I hit send. I had just written an entire book on obedience and saying yes to God, but the funny thing is God wasn't done asking yet.

It wasn't until the first-grade class Christmas party a week later that I saw the new curly-haired, redheaded mom quietly crocheting the teacher's gift in the corner of the room. I remember thinking as she whipped up a coffee mug cozy as though it was no big deal, *Well, that's cool. And different.*

It hit me that this must be the new mom with the two adopted Ethiopian boys. I made a beeline for her and probably scared her half to death with all my questions. I had just returned from Kenya, and I was hungry for someone who understood the challenge of living in one place and serving in another. Jessica was tentative with her answers, but I learned that their plans to live in Ethiopia as missionaries and serve impoverished women had been interrupted. I could see the pain in her eyes from her untold story. I was eager to get to know this new friend.

As we cleaned up the Christmas party I casually mentioned, "Hey, after the holidays, I'm going into Houston to help my friends who are teaching a class to refugees. We need someone who knows how to crochet. Want to come?"

Tears filled her eyes and she nodded her head yes.

Yes. It was a word I thought I was done saying. Because surely after you write a book about saying yes to God, he stops asking. Right? But when our Russian friends, refugees themselves, invited me to visit a class they had started to help refugee women relocated to Houston, I couldn't say no. They knew of the work we were doing in Kenya to teach skills to teen moms, and they said there was a need right here. I remember thinking, *How much need can there be here in Texas?* But when my friend told me in her accented English that refugee women were reusing disposable diapers because they couldn't afford new ones, I knew I had to go with them. These friends had been so instrumental in our lives, and to this day I want to be a part of what they are doing for the kingdom of God.

The location of the class was an hour drive from my front door, and on the way my Russian friend explained that more than fifty thousand refugees from all around the world have been relocated from refugee camps by the United Nations. When I walked into the crowded apartment clubhouse, basically a three-bedroom apartment, every sense was overwhelmed. I stepped into another culture. Some of the women were dressed in clothes from their home countries of Nepal, Bhutan, and Burma. The air smelled of spices and food I didn't recognize, but that didn't stop my stomach from rumbling. Noisy conversations in different languages were happening all over the room. It felt as though I had just entered another country, and my eyes filled with tears. It made me homesick for the women I worked with in Kenya who had turned my life upside down.

I observed and learned so much that day. Most of the women had come directly from a camp, and the United Nations tries to resettle them by country so they will have language, culture, and community in common. Though they were given $950 to start their lives in America, they struggled to make ends meet in a foreign country with a language they didn't know. I met a woman who lived in a two-bedroom apartment with twelve other relatives, and I wondered how she and her family would ever pay the UN back for the plane tickets to the United States. I didn't know how I was going to help them, but I knew I had fallen in love that day and that God was asking again.

At the time I was already stretched too thin. We didn't have any full-time Mercy House employees, and Terrell was working forty to fifty hours a week at his corporate America job so I could continue to volunteer my time running Mercy House. The last thing I had time for was a weekly class an hour from home with another group of women.

Terrell said as much to me in bed that night when I told him about visiting the refugee apartment complex. "Kristen, you're going to burn out. How can you add anything else to your plate?"

I turned toward him and said, "Honey, I can't explain it. I can only ask you to trust me. I don't know what God wants me to do, but he is asking me to go back to that apartment complex. I just turned in a manuscript about saying yes to God. I can't say no because for me this is about obedience."

Some of the refugee women knew how to knit. It seemed a good place to start. I bought a few looms, and my kids and I taught ourselves to knit with the help of a YouTube video.

Jessica and I got to know each other on our drives down to the refugee apartment. I needed someone who knew what to do with yarn, and she needed something to do with her hands. Over time Jessica shared her story of how she and her family had given up everything to move to Ethiopia to teach women skills to help them with empowerment and employment. Just six months after they moved to Africa with their three young kids, the founder of the organization they worked with was unexpectedly arrested and imprisoned. Their family had three hours to pack what they could and flee Ethiopia. They didn't know it would be the last time they would see their home.

Every Friday we dropped our kids off at school, hit the road with a trunk full of yarn, and cried our way to the heart of Houston. We didn't always know what we were doing, but we knew God had us in this place for a reason. There were many tears, fears, and dreams shared in our minivans. It was holy work; we didn't know God was beginning the birthing process again.

I approached a friend from church whom I knew to be generous about this little refugee class, and I asked him to invest $5,000 so that we could buy product from the women, sell it on their behalf, and then buy more. Our friend sowed good seed into our idea, and we started selling what the women made everywhere we could.

I was eager to introduce my family to my new refugee friends. On a hot February day in Texas, that's exactly what I did. We had only a handful of volunteers, but hundreds of needy refugees had already formed a line so everyone had a job, even our children.

From across the parking lot I watched Madison give directions to the littlest of the volunteers, who were in charge of the mound of toiletry and hygiene items we were passing out to refugees in the city. Some divided the donated supplies into more than one hundred paper sacks, while others sorted donations, led refugee families around the free garage sale, and collected their vouchers for needed items. Our kids worked for hours and never complained.

Earlier in the weekend I had felt guilty for roping my family into all this extra work. What started out as a simple yes ended up being a time-consuming, several-day event that eventually became its own nonprofit, The Refugee Project. Volunteers helped us organize and sort a truckload of donations spread out on our driveway. Madison and Jon-Avery were in the eighth and sixth grades at the time, and when they got off the school bus their friends asked if we were hoarders.

I think that might be called junior-high persecution.

As I watched my kids, who had worked hard in preparation for that day, jump in and serve refugees and navigate the language barrier, I realized they didn't need an apology for not making the weekend fun and filled with more stuff just for them and all about them! They reminded me that a bit of hard work is healthy and good for us and that it is rewarding to serve other people.

As parents, I think we've missed something important in our culture. In an effort to make family a priority and give our kids what we didn't have, we've become a child-focused culture. In many ways we've lost our purpose. The sense of entitlement our kids exhibit is fueled by a parenting model that is obsessed with giving our children what they want and with making our kids the center of our lives.

I looked at my exhausted, dirty children as they gobbled down sandwiches in the car on the way home after our full day of serving—grinning, silly and content with the busy day—and I didn't feel bad at all. I realized I had given them something money couldn't buy, something more valuable than the latest technology or hottest-brand offering. I had given them perspective and an opportunity to see their world a little differently.

During this season of running Mercy House and attending the Friday refugee class, I woke up Terrell one night because I hadn't been able to sleep. "Honey, are you awake?" I asked as I tapped his arm.

"I am now," he said groggily.

"Terrell, I can't sleep. I think God wants us to provide jobs for women." I just had to say the words out loud that had been hammering around in my heart for months.

"Kristen, aren't we doing enough? How much more can we take on?" he asked honestly. I didn't know the answer to that question, but I knew God was asking a completely different one.

Terrell was worried about me, and he had every right to be. I was pushing myself and was exhausted, and he was trying to protect me. We were still six months away from getting to the place where he could quit his job and move into the role of CEO of Mercy House. It was another scary yes that we were anticipating in the future. Terrell was making my work possible by being faithful in his, so I tried not to add to his burden.

On one fateful Friday I talked to Jessica about it because I knew she felt the pressure to provide work as I did. She understood the burden of having people in another country depend on you.

"Hey, I have an idea. We have an abundance of fair-trade product from the maternity homes in Kenya, and now we also have refugee-knitted and crocheted items. I keep thinking we should start some kind of recurring membership where we send people fair-trade product every month. Every month would be a surprise, but it would be fun and would provide jobs for these women we are trying to help."

Jessica wasn't the first person I shared this idea with, but she was the first person who said, "Yes! Let's do it. And let's call it Fair Trade Friday since we help women on Fridays." She and her husband, Keith, donated suitcases of beautiful fair-trade product they had escaped Ethiopia with to go into our first boxes. They created Excel spreadsheets and helped to procure and pack product. Our families joined forces to launch something new. That little nagging idea I couldn't shake became Fair Trade Friday, a ministry of Mercy House. That first month we had eighty members; now we have more than three thousand. Fair Trade Friday is a monthly subscription club providing jobs for thousands of women in twenty-five countries and delivering cute fair-trade product to generous women in North America. It's more than a club; it's sweet redemption.

When I look back, there wasn't one easy day during those long months. It was hard work, and it pulled and stretched our family in different directions. But it was just for a season, and we look back now and see that God was doing something good for his glory: he was bringing redemption. He redeemed broken dreams and answered prayers. He provided a way for us to provide much-needed jobs to desperate women around the world in Jesus's name. He took us through hard places so that we could make his glory known.

During this challenging season my kids weren't just watching us; they were active participants. Giving our lives away will cost us everything. When we raise world changers, we are asking them to pay that high price too. As a family we sacrificed our time, money, and resources, and in losing our lives we discovered them. We have followed Jesus into difficult places, and it is not always easy. On more than one occasion our kids have said, "But we're doing this for Jesus. Why is it so hard?" as if that's the ticket to an easier path. It's a lie our culture of comfort tries to sell us. This path won't always be easy, but it won't be empty either. Jesus reminds us in Mark 8 that we aren't alone when we follow him:

> Calling the crowd to join his disciples, he said, "Anyone who intends to come with me has to let me lead. You're not in the driver's seat; *I* am. Don't run from suffering; embrace it. Follow me and I'll show you how. Self-help is no help at all. Self-sacrifice is the way, my way, to saving yourself, your true self. What good would it do to get everything you want and lose you, the real you? What could you ever trade your soul for?" (vv. 34–37)

More than once we read the story of Joseph to our kids, and our anthem became *we are where we are for a reason.* Sometimes God puts us in a place we don't want to be in because it's the right place for us to show his glory. He uses our discomfort to forge something deep within us. God uses our pain to forge a path—a bridge—for others to find him.

Genesis 45 reveals that Joseph, a man of passion and integrity who walked in justice, was a slave for a purpose: "It was to save lives that God sent me ahead of you" (v. 5 NIV). I think Joseph would have loved John Piper's advice: "Occasionally weep deeply over the life you hoped would be. Grieve the losses. Then wash your face. Trust God. And embrace the life you have."[1]

We are talking about God's sovereignty here. He might imposition us to position us. He puts us in places that are hard, uncomfortable, and heartbreaking for a reason. God doesn't always prevent suffering; he often allows it in his sovereign plan. We may not always see his plan, but we can trust that he is only and always good. And we can believe that he is able to redeem anything—even the worst suffering. He allowed his Son to be murdered because he saw the complete picture. He knew it would bring ultimate redemption. We can trust that God is with us in the difficult places. When we face roadblocks, dead ends, heartbreak, or suffering, we can trust this: it's either for our sake or for someone else's. We may never understand why God allows what he does, but we can know it's for his glory.

As parents we might be in a place we wish we weren't—a job we despise, a home we hate, a season that is hard. Or even worse—and more out of our control—our kids might be in a place we don't like or understand. It's okay even if it doesn't feel okay because this is what's generally called *life*, and God is still in charge even when we don't like where we are. I was in one of these seasons in 2016 when I listened to the live streaming of David Platt speaking at the IF Gathering on making disciples. It was passionately delivered and deeply moving. It stopped me dead in my tracks because it reminded me of my purpose as a parent, as a Christ follower. Everything comes down to the one job God left us to accomplish on this earth—to make disciples: "Go therefore and make disciples of all nations, baptizing them in the name of the Father and of the Son and of the Holy Spirit, teaching them to observe all that I have commanded you. And behold, I am with you always, to the end of the age" (Matt. 28:19–20 ESV).

This is our purpose: to love God, love others, and make disciples. This might just be the reason we are in a place we don't like. This might be the reason we live on a particular street, our kids are in a certain school, our lives are intertwined with difficult people and daily challenges. It isn't about us; it's about trusting that God has us in this place, in this situation to make disciples. It's the ultimate act of generosity: to look up and around us and see that the purpose behind our pain is his great plan. While listening to David's sermon on John 17 that day in 2016, I wrote down the following notes:

1. Recognize the unique place in which God has put you: this season, this hard place, this valley, this mountaintop.
2. Realize what is at stake in the lives of those around you: your children who are looking to you to lead, your neighbors, friends, community, and world who are counting on you to do something.
3. Remember the simple purpose God has given you: to make disciples.[2]

When we do these three things, they make us want to share what we have. Doing so will change our family in incredible ways. Generosity is a tangible way for us to help our kids see someone other than themselves.

Start
WORLD-CHANGING
CONVERSATIONS
with Your Kids

I asked my daughter Emerson to answer the following questions. I hope they lead to good conversations with your kids.

1. Do you think God puts us in a place for a reason? Like in a certain class at school or a neighborhood? Yes, because God has a plan for each and every person, and everyone has a different plan and life. As I read my mom's words, I wondered, What if Avery and I had never met? Would Fair Trade Friday even exist? God can use anyone, even a couple of first graders.

2. Why do you think God brought your friend Avery (who wears paper beads) back to the United States from Ethiopia? I think God brought Avery back so that her mom could help my mom start Fair Trade Friday. God took a bad circumstance and made good out of it. He knew that together our moms would change the world and that I needed a good friend.

3. When life is hard and we are struggling, do you think God knows and cares? Why do you think he lets us go through hard things? Yes, I know he cares because he loves us. He can take hard things and turn them into good. He lets us go through hard things to teach us to hold on to him and to show us that he has our best interests at heart. He wants us to trust him and give all our worries and problems to him.

Practice
GENEROSITY

- Make stone soup with friends. Stone soup is based on the old folklore in which hungry strangers convince the people of a town to share small amounts of food that will create a meal for the whole town to enjoy. Ask everyone to bring one ingredient and put them all together to make a delicious meal and then have dinner together.

- Teens love clothes. Talk about the idea of giving two things away for every new item they add to their closet.

- Get your family out of their comfort zone on a regular basis. Whether it is through travel or trying new things, getting out of our comfort zone changes our perspective and helps us to see others instead of only ourselves.

7

Why We Keep Paying the Price

Joy is a sign of generosity. When you are full of joy,
you move faster and you want to go about
doing good for everyone.

Mother Teresa

I wish I could tell you his real name. There's something powerful about knowing a person's name and saying it aloud. It helps us not to forget it. But I can't tell you. It's weighty knowing that so many details about our dear Russian friends could place them in danger. Instead I will tell you his American name: John.

John is a refugee from a Muslim, Russian-speaking country where it is illegal to be a Christian. Every time I hear his story of faith and about the persecution and the humiliation he endured because of it, I weep. His family's story intersected our family's story nearly ten years ago, and the fabric of who we are and what we do has flowed from the crossroads of this relationship. Since that fateful day when our families met at a local park (we are where we are for a reason), just months after the United Nations gave them sanction in my town, we have forged a deep and meaningful relationship that has turned friends into family.

John has been imprisoned for his faith again and again, in fact, so many times that when I asked him how many he could not give me a number other than *dozens*. He was beaten for the gospel many times and humiliated in ways he would not say. He was isolated from his underground faith community. His family members were kidnapped because he could not, no, *he would not* stop telling people about Jesus. He was banished from his home and country and lost everything he possessed—house, cars, business—everything in just twenty-four hours. He was separated from his wife and small children for agonizing weeks. He was forced to start over with refugee status in America and to live by faith. Today, he still chooses every day to risk his safety and comfort to spend the rest of his life telling people about Jesus in extremely dangerous places. My children have been raised in the shadow of this hero of our faith, and his life makes me ask one question: *Why?* Why does someone risk giving everything—even their life—away for the cause of Jesus?

I can think of only one reason—joy.

Our friend John takes James 1:2–4 to heart: "Consider it pure joy, my brothers and sisters, whenever you face trials of many kinds, because you know that the testing of your faith produces perseverance. Let perseverance finish its work so that you may be mature and complete, not lacking anything" (NIV). I love the way the Message translates verses 2–3, "Consider it a sheer gift, friends, when tests and challenges come at you from all sides. You know that under pressure, your faith-life is forced into the open and shows its true colors."

This kind of joy gives great delight because it provides deep satisfaction in our souls. When we are satisfied with Jesus, we stop searching for things to fill us. When we give, instead of feeling empty we are filled. I've seen people in abject poverty in unthinkable conditions give all they have. Several years ago I sat in a home in Ethiopia and ate the last bit of food a young mother had in her house. She didn't give because she could afford it; she gave because it gave her joy to share what she'd been given. She taught me that when we depend on Jesus for everything—even our next meal—it doesn't matter what we have or don't have. Jesus makes what we have enough because he is enough.

John and his sweet wife are raising their children in America now. It isn't their first choice. Even after all these years, they miss their home, their extended family, and their country. But God placed them here for a reason, and they are living full of joy, sharing what they have with everyone they meet. Their children have nearly lost their Russian accents, although they are fluent in their native language. Their oldest daughter, whom we'll call Sarah, knows that around the globe and in the country she was born in are thousands of families worshiping God in secret because it's against the law to assemble with other believers publicly. If they are caught they face beating and imprisonment and even death. She knows this because it is her parents' story.

But she doesn't remember this life. She smiles her dimpled grin and her long braid falls over her shoulder as she tells me: "I love America. This is home." She was just three years old when her family found safety in the United States as religious refugees. Now as US citizens they lead a global movement to spread the gospel in dozens of countries.

"I don't remember much about my first home, but I do remember seeing children in poverty," Sarah says. And this memory coupled with a new life in America caused her family to sponsor two Compassion International children in Africa more than five years ago. "My brother and I use the pocket change we earn by doing chores to sponsor kids in Uganda." But they're not stopping there. "I want to sponsor more kids because I enjoy seeing how happy they are with my help, and I want them to be as happy as I am. They don't have all the things we have, and I want to give them something they need," she explains compassionately.

Giving is central to the life of a Christian. It's a tenet of our faith, the foundation God revealed to us through his ultimate act of generosity when he gave his only Son. So it makes me wonder, *If we aren't giving are we truly joyful?*

The ministry of Mercy House is fulfilling, gut-wrenching work for our family. Part of that work introduces us to selfless people who work in hard places in very difficult situations. My kids are growing up as eyewitnesses to this beautiful, brutal space. The one thing that splits my soul wide open is the stunning obedience we have seen in these selfless people—people like John and his family. We see them count the cost and continue to give, not because they are being paid well or becoming known; it's quite the opposite. They continue to give because the more they give the deeper their joy.

On our last family trip to Kenya, we visited the homes of several women we are working to help. One of the homes we will never forget was that of a young mother from the Street Hope artisan group we began in 2016. The group is composed of mothers—most of them still teenagers—who were homeless. They lived on the streets and survived by begging during the day and prostituting at night, all with babies strapped on their backs.

Slowly, one by one, these women learned to sew by hand and began making tiny felt hearts for fair-trade tic-tac-toe games we sold in America. It's surprising to think something so small could have such a big impact, but these little hearts (and the big heart of God) changed their lives. We walked the path to one such young mother's home, following the stream of sewage that eventually led to a river of waste. The deeper you go into a slum, the worse the conditions get. But that didn't stop her from beaming that day as she showed us her little house next to the river of sewage. She was proud to have a home.

As my family crowded onto her couch, the only furniture in the home besides a bed, she told us her story. "I am an orphan. I have been on the street alone since I was nine years old. I did whatever I could to survive. I was pregnant by age eleven. This is my son," she said as she hugged her flailing eight-year-old boy, who was nearly as tall as she was. Due to her age and size, he had been born too early and was severely handicapped as a result.

I looked at my family. We were all crying. Terrell's shoulders shook as he silently sobbed. I was pretty sure it had something to do with our ten-year-old in his lap. This was a true story, and it was simply unthinkable. At just nineteen, HIV positive, and the mother of an eight-year-old, she had already lived such a cruel life.

"I have been alone my entire life. Until now," she said as she started crying. Our family, along with our Kenyan directors, put our arms around her and we cried together.

I have had many conversations with my kids about the hopelessness we witness and what it does deep in your soul; it begs you to bring hope. Showing our kids the brokenness in our world breaks them, but this is how they learn compassion. It's how the needs of the world become needs of their own. It's how they become a part of someone else's story.

Before we left we looked into the beautiful, dark eyes of this young woman, and we made her a promise: *hope is on the way.* We returned home desperate to do something to provide hope in the form of jobs for her and the other women we had visited. We made phone calls and hired teachers. We rented a small room in a central location so these women would have a place to "go to work." We stepped out in faith because we believe that God wants us to share what we have with people who have less.

Two weeks later I sat in a hotel room working on the book you hold in your hands. The next morning I woke up to an email that outlined the budget for a kiln, two looms, and supplies. To bring hope would cost $5,100. I cried at the overwhelming number. As a nonprofit ministry, our budget is always bigger than our pockets because the need to empower women in poverty and oppression is priceless. And the more women you help, the more women need to be helped. And the more you give, the deeper you're drawn into generosity.

As I sat alone in that hotel room, crying and wondering how I would continue to write when I felt so heavy, I put this on my Facebook status: "I woke up to a need in Kenya to provide looms and a kiln and supplies. Maybe someone woke up with a desire to meet it?"

Fifteen minutes later I got this text from a wildly generous sister who has given and given and given some more because she is addicted to the profound joy that comes when you give your life away: "My family would like to provide looms and a kiln and pottery glazes."

The dam broke. Hope was on the way. I didn't just cry, I wailed. I called my family from that hotel room and bawled into the phone. And it wasn't just my joy. It was our joy because they knew of the need for jobs, and they rejoiced when the miracle came. My kids had witnessed the hopelessness, and they needed to see the hope as badly as I did.

In the next text my friend continued with these stunning words: "God doesn't call us to a convenient life—he calls us to an important life. . . . We aren't meant for self-gratification, but eternal greatness . . . and greatness is giving our lives away. Thank you for giving us a chance to serve with you, Kristen. You and Terrell are a gift to us! Maybe someday I can sit at some looms and by some kilns and hear how God has made miracles happen—and we will tell those stories, sister."

Oh, I'm glad there wasn't an eyewitness to the unleashing of my joy that day in the hotel room. I was quite loud, and there was a lot of snot. The words on my phone and the money in the mail were messages from God himself to my family: *This is working. This crazy idea to provide dignified jobs for women as a road to the gospel is working. Because I am working. Keep giving and I'll keep filling you with unparalleled joy.*

One of the greatest joys in my life is getting to live out my purpose in front of my kids. Terrell and I were talking the other night before bed about how we cannot wait to get to work every day. We cannot wait to see what God will do. We get to live out this adventure and witness the miraculous, and our children are eyewitnesses to his holiness and what he can do with regular people.

Kids are our toughest critics. One time we asked them to grade us on our parenting in various areas, and we barely passed. We never did that again! When our children see God do something extraordinary with our generosity, we don't impress them (they know our weaknesses, remember?). They don't see us—they see Jesus.

According to a *Focus on the Family* article titled, "Raising a Cheerful Giver: Teaching Children to Give Generously," "Researchers seeking to understand the roots of compassion and generosity have sought answers from a much-celebrated group of heroes: those who risked everything to rescue Jews from the horrors of the Holocaust." The article then cites Jan Johnson's book *Growing Compassionate Kids*. She summarizes the findings of Doug Huneke, who wrote a biography of Hermann "Fritz" Graebe and conducted interviews with three hundred others who rescued Jews during World War II. Huneke identifies ten traits these individuals had in common:

1. A history of overcoming challenges in childhood
2. The influence of a morally strong parent or grandparent
3. A past experience of being marginalized or considered an "outsider"
4. Strong empathy
5. Strong powers of persuasion
6. A cooperative attitude and a sense of responsibility for others
7. Exposure to suffering at an early age
8. The ability to examine their own prejudices
9. Belonging to a community who valued compassion
10. A home life characterized by hospitality.[1]

What an amazing list! It's inspiring to think we are raising kids who really can change the world.

Joy isn't reserved just for people with money. We don't have to be rich to be generous. I love this quote by Timothy L. Smith, author of *Donors Are People Too*: "Generosity is not something that comes later after you accumulate wealth. It's something you live out wherever you are in life today. It's not something that 'shows up'—it's a lifestyle you cultivate."[2]

While I respect the work of Dave Ramsey, who encourages people to get out of debt and live debt free, I have always taken issue with his principle that we should live in such a way that later we can give like no one else. He encourages people to "give like no one else" *after* they have saved and accumulated wealth. This is well and good, but I don't believe God wants us to wait until we have wealth. There is no "later" in terms of the gospel. There is only now. How else can we cultivate a life of giving? Giving is not a lifestyle we adopt when we have money; giving starts today. It's something we teach our kids today. Given the fact that Americans are among the richest people in the world, we have to live like no one else (that is, not chasing the American dream) and begin right now where we are to give like no one else.

Even those in poverty can raise kids to be generous because the root of generosity isn't wealth. The root of generosity is compassion, empathy, humility, and a strong work ethic. It's teaching our kids to share what they've been given—their time, talents, and resources. Sometimes generosity looks like giving money away, but sometimes it looks like the child of a Russian refugee giving piano lessons so she can sponsor more children. Instilling these qualities and characteristics into our kids not only makes them generous but also leads them to satisfying joy.

I can't tell you my refugee friend's real name, but I can tell you his words. After sharing his powerful testimony with a group of my friends in the nonprofit world, he closed with these heart-stopping words: "Christians are bored with Christianity and their lives because they are just reading the stories in the Bible. But I don't want to just read and hear the stories. I want to live them. I want to be in the epicenter of what God is doing. There are people today—in China, the Middle East, and around the world—living the stories of the Bible—right now, at this moment. The cure for boredom requires us to step into spaces that are out of our control." And then he urged us with these countercultural words that I will never forget: "Do not invest your life on things you can lose in twenty-four hours."

How do we take these prophetic words and let them sink into our everyday lives? How do we let them shape who we are, how we parent, and ultimately, how we live? We can

- *Give thanks for what we have.* Twice this week I've met people who are risking everything they have—even their lives—so that others may have Jesus, someone we take for granted.

- *Invest our lives in more than the American dream.* In twenty-four hours, all we have can disappear. Let's spend our lives and our money helping people. It's an eternal investment.

- *Refuse to live a bored Christian life.* Let's get involved in God's work where and when we can. There are people right now losing their lives because of their Christian faith.

Every year we host a giving day for Mercy House called She Is Priceless (sheispriceless.org). But we don't raise money just for *our* work of empowering women globally; we also raise money for other groups doing the same thing. In the world of fund-raising, doing this might seem like we are missing the point because it certainly divides the money we need rather than multiply it. But that's only one way to look at it. We take a different approach: we are becoming a part of another organization's story. We are linking arms with them and saying we believe in what you do so much that we want our people to know about it too. And we are able to step into spaces and go to places we've never been because we are telling their story along with ours. We are doing it because of joy. When their ministry needs are met, impoverished and oppressed women are helped in Jesus's name, and that brings us all joy. The lesson I want to teach my kids is this: when we give to others we aren't subtracting from our own joy, we are multiplying it.

Start
WORLD-CHANGING
CONVERSATIONS
with Your Kids

I asked my daughter Madison to answer the following questions. I hope they lead to good conversations with your kids.

1. If we are here on this earth to glorify God, how do we do that? I think glorifying God starts with a simple prayer every single day in which we ask God to use us and help us glorify his name in everything we do. Like many things, this principle takes practice and diligence; we will mess up, and that's okay. But the thing that helps us glorify God is to keep trying. We will make mistakes; it's guaranteed. But we have to choose to keep trying and to keep asking God to help us. Glorifying God is a daily choice in which we choose to do things for his glory instead of our own. We continually use the opportunities he gives us to point back to him and to share his name. Many people think that in order to glorify God you need to be like John, starting global movements and literally changing the world. However, God has put us right where we are for a reason and an important purpose. So how can we glorify God? By doing what he has called us to do right where he has called us, and by doing it for his glory and his glory alone.

2. How do we find our purpose? I think this is a tough question for anyone, but especially for me! I have wrestled with this question for a long time and have truly tried to seek out my purpose in this life. However, I think that I often overcomplicate things. When I think of the word purpose it seems like this one, big, extremely important quest that we have for our lives. Many people spend their entire lives trying to find their purpose. But if we go back to the Bible we easily find the answer. God tells us to simply go and do. As Christians we are called to go into all the nations and spread the good news. These were Jesus's last and most important words. Our purpose in life is simply to love the people around us and tell them about Jesus. God has given each of us unique and amazing gifts and has placed us right where we are for a reason. He doesn't make mistakes. You and I are right where we are in this exact stage of life because we are called to go and do. This purpose doesn't change as our lives change; we are continually called to go and do. So I think in order to find our purpose we simply do what God is calling us to do. We go and do and trust that he will help us figure out the rest.

3. Do you think serving others can help us accomplish the first two questions? Why? I think serving others directly relates to glorifying God and finding our purpose. When we serve others, we are doing what God has called us to do. We are going and doing, and we are glorifying him. Jesus was the greatest example of what being a servant and serving look like, and in our lives today his example is still relevant. As Christians we can glorify God and fulfill our purpose by simply serving those around us in every way that we can. Not all of us are called to Africa or to start global movements, but we are all called to go and do and to glorify God. No matter where we are in life we can accomplish these two things simply by seeing a need around us and filling it through service to others.

Practice

GENEROSITY

- Create an opportunity for your kids to learn empathy. If they've never experienced the "new kid" feeling, give them the opportunity by teaching them how to start conversations with people they don't know or by allowing them to order food for themselves. This will help them to grow in courage. Families that move often experience this "outsider" feeling, and it makes them very aware when their peers feel it. They will be the first ones to welcome a new kid to school or sit with a loner at lunch.

- Show your kids a tangible need by taking them to a local nonprofit that helps the homeless. Ask if your family can sort clothes or prepare meals. Or visit a nursing home and bring coloring books and crayons. Sit with the elderly and invite them to color or to receive a picture. It's natural to want to protect our kids from extremes, but it's not always beneficial. Empathy and compassion are ignited when we come face-to-face with suffering.

- Play this "refugee experience" game with them: give each child nine slips of paper and tell them to write down three things they love, three people they love, and three titles they have (daughter, son, student, or grandchild, for example). Ask them to choose one slip of paper from each group and throw it away.

Talk with them about how difficult the decisions were for them to make. Next, take one slip of paper from each others' piles without looking at it. Talk about what's left and compare their feelings to how modern-day refugees feel when they lose their identity, possessions, and even family by having to flee for their lives.

8

The Happiest People Alive

There is more happiness in giving than in receiving.

Acts 20:35 GNT

I remember the first time I saw the picture on my husband's phone. I cringed and tried to grab it from him. He held it over my head as I reached for it. "Is that your profile picture? Why did you choose that picture? I hadn't had a shower in days and look at my hair! It's a terrible picture of me."

I thought back to the day it was taken. I was in Kenya without my family, and our staff was visiting a home in one of the poorest areas in the city. There was nothing happy about the setting: there was no roof over our head, no kitchen, and no bathroom. I was sitting on a rock, the only furniture in the house, with a dirt floor under my feet and talking to the family of a girl we had rescued. I was scared, dirty, homesick, and overwhelmed, but I was at peace because I knew I was exactly where I was supposed to be and doing exactly what I was created to do. When the photographer snapped my picture in that setting, she captured both the harsh background and the joy on my face. Terrell laughed at my vanity and simply said, "This is my new favorite photo of you. I've never seen you look more beautiful. I made it my profile picture because it's the happiest I've ever seen you."

For years that picture was my profile picture too. My kids got used to seeing it. We didn't see a mom who needed to wash her hair; we saw an expression of pure joy. Our culture is obsessed with beauty and happiness, and we will pay any price to try to grasp them. I've seen my kids, especially my daughters, struggle to separate beauty and happiness and understand this truth: beautiful people aren't always the happiest, but happy people are always the most beautiful.

It's just a matter of time before our kids are sucked into this happiness-seeking vortex. Once when I was together with an old friend I corrected my strong-willed child for bad behavior in front of her while hers got away with the very same thing. She said, "I find that my child is a lot happier when I just give in." We eventually stopped getting together after that because I couldn't compete with her "happy" child who was also often bratty.

I was a young mom, but I realized right then and there that a child who is happy in the near term isn't always a healthy one in the long term. I am not anti-happy. I don't purposefully make my kids sad or angry. I do think it's important to stick to my guns, and unhappiness often flows from that. When children are unhappy it generally means we as parents are doing something right. Their unhappiness is often a result of us trying to shape

124

their wills into ours and ultimately into God's. My goal is deeper than happiness. I'm after contentment. I think any parent who deals with unhappy kids probably gets the reality of Proverbs 15:13 very well: "A happy heart makes the face cheerful" (NIV). True happiness comes from within. While grumpy faces are quite common, sometimes they are the result of a heart matter.

I'm convinced generous people are the happiest. I think most people would agree that giving makes them feel happy. A series of studies conducted by Harvard Business School professor Michael Norton and two of his colleagues found that "giving money to someone else lifted participants' happiness more than spending it on themselves (despite participants' prediction that spending on themselves would make them happier)."[1] Norton said, "We found that people who spent the money on themselves that day weren't happier that evening, but people who spent it on others were. The amount of money, $5 or $20, didn't matter at all. It was only how people spent it that made them happier."[2]

I love that even science is a fan of giving. I ran across this 2006 study by Jorge Moll and colleagues at the National Institutes of Health who found that "when people give to charities, it activates regions of the brain associated with pleasure, social connection, and trust, creating a 'warm glow' effect. Scientists also believe that altruistic behavior releases endorphins in the brain, producing the positive feeling known as the 'helper's high.'"[3]

Giving not only makes us happier people but also has numerous other health benefits. It reduces stress, lowers blood pressure, makes us less depressed, and might even help us live longer![4] It can improve our marriage and relationships, according to a 2017 study by researchers at the University of Rochester:

125

"Compassionate concern for others' welfare enhances one's own affective state."[5]

Some of the most profound research on the correlation between happiness and generosity is found in *The Paradox of Generosity* by Christian Smith and Hilary Davidson. The following quote sums up well the outcome of the research: "Rather than leaving generous people on the short end of an unequal bargain, practices of generosity are actually likely instead to provide generous givers with essential goods in life—happiness, health, and purpose—which money and time themselves simply cannot buy. That is an empirical fact well worth knowing."[6]

If scientific research and facts don't impress you, happiness produced by generosity is also a biblical principle. Giving of our time, talents, and resources brings satisfaction and deep contentment. James 1:17 reminds us that "every good gift and every perfect gift is from above, coming down from the Father of lights with whom there is no variation or shadow due to change" (ESV). He gives because he loves us, and he offers us an example of how we should live.

True contentment is being okay with life whether you get your way or not. When my daughter wants another new pair of shoes or the latest scarf to add to her collection, I usually *want* to give it to her and that would certainly make her happy (for the time being). But since my ultimate goal is to reduce entitlement, feed gratitude, and produce contentment, I don't automatically buy it for her. While I do sometimes buy my kids things just because I want to, I don't always, and this alone can produce temporary unhappiness. I often make them save, work, or wait for it, and occasionally I treat them after they've worked hard for something they've had their eye on.

I love the truth of this pointed statement from Dr. Kevin Leman: "Did you know that your job as a parent is not to create a happy child? That if your child is temporarily unhappy, when he or she does choose to put a happy face back on, life will be better for all of you?"[7]

We live in a culture that is terrified of raising unhappy kids. We overindulge, cater to every whim, and often let them grow up much faster than they need to. When the Bible talks about trials and tribulations testing our faith and making it stronger, that's not intended only for adults. It's for believers. Some of the best lessons my kids have learned are through their own personal hardships (a fashion crisis, for example, can be a hardship to a preteen girl). So when our kiddos are pouting and mumbling and seem unhappy, *take heart*—you are doing a good job and ultimately raising healthy adults.

The truth is life can be hard. There are unexpected detours in our journeys that are heartbreaking and difficult to process. If we don't understand this, we can't possibly teach it to our children. We were created to be satisfied by God, not by this world, so all this searching for happiness will only lead us to unhappiness. This became especially clear when my family and I sat in a Bible study and listened to the prayer requests around the room. I caught myself thinking about the difference between first- and third-world prayers, and I wondered what in the world God must think? In one part of the world I've witnessed people begging God for provision for one more day, and here at home I've listened to good church folk asking God for more, more, more—not realizing how much they already have. God created all and loves each of us completely, but if one group isn't helping the other (and both need help), I don't know what we are really doing here.

I quickly swallowed down any judgmental thoughts because I knew these good people were just like me—one minute wanting to change the world and the next being changed by it.

We are so distracted by our culture of plenty that we feed ourselves all we can, yet we walk away empty and unsatisfied. Jon-Avery noticed the depth of the prayer requests too and mentioned it to me. He took it a step further and said, "Mom, it seems like even Christians try to fill their lives with stuff, and no matter how much they have, they want more." He was referring to friends who live in a stunning home, and their prayer request was about selling it to build a better one. It's confusing. We talked about it for a while, and I reminded him that distraction was one of the tools of our greatest enemy. And even though it might look different in our lives, we were guilty too.

A few days before that Bible study I had taken my kids into Houston, now the most diverse city in the United States, and we spent the day welcoming an Iraqi family from a refugee camp to Houston. I learned that many of the single moms being resettled in my city were also at great risk of being trafficked because they couldn't take care of their babies and work a regular job. It shook me to the core, and I desired to do something to provide these women with jobs through Mercy House because that's what we do.

If the "wanting to do something" was the same as "doing something," we would all be Mother Teresa. But somewhere between the *want to* and the *follow through* we are often distracted by our own first-world problems. That same week we had pipes break, toilets overflow, a retainer eaten by a dog, and cars in repair, and before you knew it I was preaching to the choir and my *want to* fell off by the wayside. But when I read these words in John 12, I wanted to follow through: "Very truly

I tell you, unless a kernel of wheat falls to the ground and dies, it remains only a single seed. But if it dies, it produces many seeds. Anyone who loves their life will lose it, while anyone who hates their life in this world will keep it for eternal life" (vv. 24–25 NIV).

J. D. Walt writes a daily devotion called Seedbed, and these words landed in my inbox in the middle of my bad week:

> We so want the Christian life to be reasonable, but it is not. To give a little or even a lot is the same as giving nothing at all. The life hid with Christ in God will be everything or it will be nothing. . . . The un-surrendered life is the same thing as the unplanted seed—a waste. Why on earth would we go another day holding on to the tiny seed of our life? It's time to sow our small, fragile selves into the field of God's dream for our lives. What if the little boy had shared his five loaves and two fish with the crowd? How far would it have gone? Exactly nowhere. Instead, look what happened when he surrendered all he had to Jesus. Precisely unimaginable. We think the Gospel is about sharing our lives with others, as though a seed could be shared. No, it's about surrendering our lives to Jesus, who will make of our lives an unending, unimaginable gift to the world. Sharing will never get it done. Only surrender will.[8]

I realized I'd been trying to convince people to share what they have been given because we have been given so much. While this is not exactly wrong, it's not what Jesus asks of us. It isn't about sharing our lives; it's about surrendering them. And what's so crazy and beautiful is that when we surrender everything, we get twice as much in return! This is the key to true happiness.

It helps us balance the good and the bad—and remain happy in either—if we believe this truth from Jennie Allen, author and founder of the IF Gathering: "If we know no place, no job, no marriage, no child is going to fulfill us perfectly, we can make the choice to quit fighting for happiness in all of it and start to fight for God's glory in it."[9] Because we can trust that God will be glorified in the mess of our lives.

Several years ago on a family trip to Kenya we participated in a local outreach as a way for the rescued teen moms to give back and remember the suffering in their city. We traveled to a home for disabled and handicapped children and spent the day serving this community. Sadly, children with special needs are often referred to as throwaways in poor areas. Many families don't have enough food for their healthy children, and a handicapped child without resources such as education or a wheelchair is sometimes abandoned or given up. We were admonished by the staff to love these children and not to let fear stop us from serving.

I won't lie; it was heartbreaking. The living conditions were difficult to absorb, and my senses were overwhelmed. My eyes burned at the putrid smell and my throat closed as we made our way from room to room on a tour of the facility. We were handed trays of food to pass out. Children came from all over the compound. Some limped on crutches and others crawled on bent and twisted limbs.

Many of the children couldn't feed themselves so we spoon-fed them. I pushed away my fear and tried to be the hands of Jesus. Mostly, I tried to follow my kids' examples. More than once, I checked to see how they were doing. I worried this was too much for them to see and experience. But every time, they assured me they were fine and even looked happy to wipe a chin and offer a plate. When Madison stood in the center of the compound to play her flute in a miniconcert, the children clapped and squealed in delight.

I don't think I've ever been more proud of my kids. They didn't flinch when the air was filled with loud screams or a child drooled on their hand as they fed them. They accepted what we saw without questions. They hugged and served the children and taught me so much.

Receiving—being the recipients of generosity—can be a little more difficult than giving. It's probably just plain old pride, but sometimes it's difficult to receive even when we are desperate for what's being given. When someone offers to bring us a meal during our busiest week of the year when we're preparing for our biggest fund-raiser, it's hard for me to accept even though I have no idea what my family will eat because I haven't had time to get to the grocery store. Or when Brittany, one of our longtime employees at Mercy House, shared with her in-laws the beauty and heartbreak of our work and her in-laws offered their beautiful home in Colorado to our family the first time, I was thrilled and a little embarrassed at my eagerness to use what wasn't mine. But I couldn't think of anything we needed more as a family than a quiet place to think, pray, rest, and be together.

That first trip to Colorado was like drinking from a deep, deep well, and it quickly became a sacred space for our family to visit each year it was available. We even named our big, furry Sheepadoodle dog Gunnison after the beautiful Rocky Mountain town.

God revealed to me that by not receiving what was being offered—a home-cooked meal, a free vacation home, and much more—that I was stopping the stunning cycle of generosity. These beautiful people were giving because it brought them joy. And when we received it, we were letting them become a part of our story. This is one of my favorite parts of this journey:

God doesn't call all of us to do everything. But when we support someone doing something that is kingdom centered, we become a part of it too.

It reminds me of the joy I feel as a parent when I see my kids give from their hearts. Madison is the best gift giver in our home. She is wildly generous, often spending too much to buy the perfect gift. Several years ago when I watched her joy one Christmas morning, I realized she wasn't giddy over what she received; she was happy about what she was giving. It was so sweet to watch her watch the faces of her siblings as they ripped open the presents she had carefully chosen and paid for with babysitting money. It cost her every cent in her purse, but it was worth it to her.

Start
WORLD-CHANGING
CONVERSATIONS
with Your Kids

I asked my daughter Madison to answer the following questions. I hope they lead to good conversations with your kids.

1. Is it better to give or to receive? Why? Of course it is always nice to receive a gift that someone thoughtfully picked out for you, but I personally think it is much better to give. As my mom said, I love to make or pick out a special gift for each of my family members when it is their birthday or Christmas or another holiday. There is nothing more fulfilling and priceless than seeing their faces when they open the gifts I picked out for them and seeing the way it makes them feel loved and cherished. I think this principle extends far beyond giving a simple present on a holiday. When we give our time, resources, money, talents, and gifts away, we feel fulfilled and truly happy. Just like there is nothing more special than seeing the face of someone you love when you give them a gift, there is nothing more fulfilling and satisfying than serving someone else and getting to see the way it impacts them and their life.

2. Most kids don't have very much money. What are some ways they can still give? I am a creative and artsy person, and I love making things with my hands. There is nothing better than giving a beautiful homemade gift to someone and using the talents God has given you to make something that someone else will enjoy. And even more than making gifts, I love the way people react when they receive them. I'm not the best at always making sure the people I love know I love them, but giving a special gift meant just for them is one way that I can do that. I love it when people make me feel special by giving me a gift that perfectly fits my personality, and I want to recreate that feeling for others.

3. What would you say to kids who don't have much money to give? For kids who don't have a lot of money to give, there are so many other things they can do. For Mother's Day one year my siblings and I decided that instead of using money we didn't have to buy our mom a gift, we would use our time and effort to show her how much we loved her. We spent all day Saturday before Mother's Day mowing the front lawn, pulling weeds, and planting flowers. This simple and seemingly "cheap" act blew our mom away and made her feel loved and appreciated. Instead of spending money on someone, show them how much you love them. Bake their favorite dessert or fix them breakfast in bed. Use your creative side and make them something you know they would love. Clean the house or plant a garden. Showing people how much we love them doesn't have to be restricted by money; serving others and using the talents and gifts God has given us is incredibly meaningful and fulfilling.

Practice
GENEROSITY

- Carve out a consistent time to read stories about how other people live. Just a chapter or a few sentences on a consistent basis will be enlightening. Our family favorites are *Running for My Life* by Lopez Lamong and *He Walks Among Us* by Richard and Reneé Stearns.

- Identify someone your family knows who could use encouragement, love, and prayer and work as a team to show that to them.

- Be the best neighbors on your block by looking for ways to serve those around you. Maybe you could pick up trash, rake leaves, start a meal train for a sick neighbor or a new mom, or coordinate a carpool. Be the house that invites the rest of the kids over!

9

What's Really at Stake?

I know that the experiences of our lives, when we let God
use them, become the mysterious and perfect preparation
for the work he will give us to do.

Corrie ten Boom

I stood in church behind her. I watched her worship, and I *knew*.

I had known Ally for a long time, but I didn't really know her.
I knew she was in her late twenties and was the first American
born to a refugee family. I knew she was amazing with kids,
and my own children fell in love with her during summer camp.
I knew she could cook delicious Thai and Laos food and that
she always had a smile on her face. But standing behind her,
listening to her sing and worship God, I knew she was supposed
to work at Mercy House.

At the time I didn't know what her skills were, but it didn't
matter because we needed employees who loved Jesus more
than we needed anything else. It didn't take long for me to

fall in love with Ally. She was not just good at her job, she was great at it because she understood that it wasn't merely work—it was ministry. She started out as our intern and in January of 2017 took a full-time position as the manager of our retail stores.

One day I commented on the fair-trade necklace she wore almost every day. It was a gold bar stamped with the words "For such a time as this." We talked about Esther and God's timing and plan. She told me she wanted to learn as much as she could because she was supposed to return to Thailand to work with impoverished and oppressed women. If I could have loved Ally more, I would have that day. I asked her to order more of the necklaces for us to sell in our store, and I wear mine almost as frequently as Ally does.

Ally started at Mercy House two weeks after that pivotal trip to New York City with Madison I mentioned earlier. One of the highlights of that trip was finally meeting Melody Murray, founder of JOYN. Mel and I had been friends for quite a while thanks to email, phone, and the power of the internet, but this was our first opportunity to encourage each other face-to-face.

When we started our monthly subscription club, Fair Trade Friday, in 2014, JOYN products quickly became a club favorite. Every gorgeous bag has quite the story, and each bag provides a total of eleven jobs—from the weaver who creates the fabric to the man who carves the stamp to the block printer who stamps the fabric to seamstress and leather maker and others—eleven jobs! Their website says, "JOYN is a socially-conscious fashion brand producing women's handbags that are 100 percent hand-made. JOYN bags aren't mass-produced. People make them. Real people with names and faces and stories and passions.

Each bag is unique. No factories, no automation, because the more hands that it takes to make the products, the more jobs we are able to create." Not only is JOYN's mission stunning, so are their bags.

In late 2015 when the Murray family had to suddenly and traumatically leave their home in the Himalayas due to the political climate, they were devastated. They had given more than five years of their lives to the cause of empowerment, but due to reasons out of their control they lost access to their home and businesses and to their friends and community, who had become family.

It's easy to lose sight of what God is doing behind the scenes when we can't see it or understand it. It's even harder when our children are impacted. Mel and I talked about this from every angle—as entrepreneurs, nonprofit leaders, and mothers. Mel and her husband, Dave, have two amazing little boys, and it was easy to identify with their heartbreak. Our family is living a life we didn't plan either, and I found great comfort and encouragement in her words when I asked about their deportation. Over the phone she shared her mother's heart with me: "My children's view of home, safety, and community changed that day. I want what most parents want for their kids. I want my boys to grow up happy and to feel cared for, safe, and peaceful. I want them to have a healthy childhood and nurturing memories. These are our instincts. But in this loss of home and our normal, I realized that I can't protect them from everything. I can try to shield them, but the world will throw tough stuff at my kids. To be honest, they handled this situation better than my husband and I did. They see evil more clearly than we do. They trust God easier.

"We do everything in our power to protect our kids from the pain of this world. It's part of our job, right? But no matter how hard we try, there is pain in life. It's tempting to avoid risks, adventure, uncertainty, and even obedience because we want to live in safety and comfort. But we end up causing more problems for our kids when we rush to resolve their conflicts and protect them from life. When we do this we raise kids who run to us for the answers instead of God."

I think of John Piper's description of the providence of God in *A Sweet and Bitter Providence*:

> Life is not a straight line leading from one blessing to the next and then finally to heaven. Life is a winding and troubled road. Switchback after switchback. And the point of biblical stories like Joseph and Job and Esther and Ruth is to help us feel in our bones (not just know in our heads) that God is for us in all these strange turns. God is not just showing up after the trouble and cleaning it up. He is plotting the course and managing the troubles with far-reaching purposes for our good and for the glory of Jesus Christ.[1]

Months later as we drank coffee at our first face-to-face meeting in the New York City Starbucks, Mel told me what she thought might be next for her family. "We are moving overseas to Southeast Asia to expand God's work of empowerment to the Golden Triangle where Thailand, Burma, and Laos join. We are making plans now and are looking for a translator."

I immediately thought of Ally. I told Mel all about her, and she agreed that they should meet. As I was talking I touched my necklace with its prophetic message, and I knew in my heart that Ally would be going with her. I already felt the loss, smiled at Ally's gain, and remembered how God is always working even when we can't see it or understand his plan. I felt as though I were sending off one of my kids, and I would be sad to see her leave. But I know God's plan is good, and he prepares us for such a time as this. It's the same dream I have for my own kids—to follow God wherever he leads. By the time you hold this book in your hands, it's entirely possible Ally and Mel's family will be living and working together in Southeast Asia.

I came home from that trip and began reading the book of Esther again. I have always loved the story of Queen Esther. Esther was forced to participate in a "beauty pageant" at the whim of a king named Xerxes in the city of Susa. The Old Testament book of Nehemiah takes place during a time of exile and captivity for the Jewish people also in the city of Susa. Perhaps their lives overlapped. Some scholars even believe it was Queen Esther who influenced the king to allow Nehemiah to rebuild the city wall.[2]

I'm inspired by these words from Raechel Myers on her blog *She Reads Truth*: "We serve a God who designs our deliverance before man can begin to devise our destruction."[3] In Esther 4 the queen learns of a plot to destroy the Jews. She is asked to approach the king and we read: "If you remain silent at this time, relief and deliverance for the Jews will arise from another place, but you and your father's family will perish. And who knows but that you have come to your royal position for such a time as this?" (v. 14 NIV). I find comfort when I remember that before an evil plot was set into motion to destroy Esther, God had already devised a way to rescue her.

We are where we are for a reason. We are called to give up our lives for the gospel. If we don't lose our lives for Christ, we will lose our souls to this world. It's not about how much we give away; it's about what we are giving our lives for. "Then [Jesus] called the crowd to him along with his disciples and said:

'Whoever wants to be my disciple must deny themselves and take up their cross and follow me'" (Mark 8:34 NIV).

Sometimes God puts us in a place we don't want to be because it's the right place for him to reveal his glory. He uses our discomfort to forge something deep within us. I love how Ann Voskamp calls us the Esther Generation. In a 2013 blog post she writes:

> You've got to use the life you've been given to give others life. If your life isn't about giving relief—you don't get real life. What does it profit a man to gain the whole world but lose his own soul?
>
> You have got to use your position inside the gate for those outside the gate—or you're in the position of losing everything. *There are a thousand ways to be the living dead.*
>
> If you have any food in your fridge, any clothes in your closet, any small roof, rented or owned, over your head, you are richer than 75% of the rest of the world. We are the Esthers living inside the palace.
>
> If you can read these words right now, you have a gift 3 billion people right now don't; if your stomach isn't twisted in hunger pangs, you have a gift that 1 billion people right now don't; if you know Christ, you have a gift that untold millions right now don't. We are the ones living inside the gate. . . .
>
> You are where you are for such a time as this—not to gain anything *but to risk everything.* You are where you are for such a time as this—not to make an impression *but to make a difference.*[4]

Do we really care about the lost and poor of the world? I have been with women who release their waste in a plastic bag without any dignity because they don't have access to a bathroom or the five cents to pay to use a filthy public one. And then they look into my eyes and ask, "Do they know how we live?" Do people in North America know how the rest of the world lives? It's the kind of gut-wrenching question that changes your life. I vow I will tell them, but I don't know if they will care.

Are we so concerned with our own self-centered lives that we don't care people are dying? Are we so obsessed with building a comfortable life that all we can offer the poor is our leftovers? Perhaps one of the biggest deceptions we believe is that what we have isn't enough to meet the overwhelming needs in the world, so maybe we should do nothing.

I think that's why I love Esther's story so much. She gave what she had and God did the rest—the impossible. God says give me what you've got. Think about the boy with his small lunch of fish and loaves in John 6. God wants what we are holding in our hands. It's small and, yes, it's not enough, but it's all God asks. He will take it and do something miraculous with it. The story is bigger than we are because the story isn't about us; it's about Jesus. It's not about what we can do; it's about what he can do. There's nothing more satisfying than giving God what we have so he can draw others to himself.

When I think about Ally and Mel, Queen Esther, and even my family, I think of ruined lives. I have this favorite pair of jeans. I've been wearing these faded denims for an embarrassingly long time. They fit just right. They are comfortable. They are trustworthy. I know them.

I used to feel that way about my life. It was predictable, comfortable, easy. It was shallow in many ways, but I knew what I was getting. It was chocolate cake—sweet though empty. My life was a safe bet.

When I woke up from the American dream in a slum in Kenya in 2010, I found soul-fulfilling purpose—that also ruined my life.

It's not sad, but it is true: when we open our eyes to those around us and step outside our comfort zone—either by choice or by life's unexpected circumstances—we will never fit back into our old lives the same way again. God didn't call only my husband and me to see the world differently and walk in obedience; he also called our family. Our choices and decisions impact our home. It's as brutal as it is beautiful. It's a glorious gutting. Some days I'm homesick for what I didn't know. I have grieved the loss of the ignorance from my former life and longed for its comfort in some weak moments. For many years now our work has been filled with trials and trauma from across the ocean to our own back door.

But I still thank God for slaying me because even in my life's toughest moments there is always someone facing something harder. Perspective saves us every time. This awakening is filled with pain and purpose, but I want to live with eyes wide open. I am weary and worn, but I am anything but empty. The second we look up from our lives to see how other people live we drink from their cup of suffering, and nothing will ever taste the same again.

Thank God, because emptiness is a bitter cup.

I pulled at the frayed hem of those familiar jeans and realized they don't quite fit anymore. That's what happens when you grow. I don't know if your life has been ruined by divorce or disease, by criticism or a calling, by death or disaster, by broken bones or broken dreams. But I do know that every moment of pain in this path to obedience is producing a peculiar and eternal glory. Though God ruins us for this life and we long for the next one, we will praise him.

God has a good plan for each of us—for such a time as this.

Generosity is really about teaching our kids to see people other than themselves. And as parents it begins with us. We have to open our eyes to the needs around us for our children to do the same. As Ann Voskamp says, "We only get one life here. It's a crazy, beautiful, liberating thing to realize: We're not here to help ourselves to more—we're here to help others to real life. We're here to live beyond our base fears because our lives are based in Christ."[5]

I asked my daughter Madison to answer the following questions. I hope they lead to good conversations with your kids.

1. How does God use pain in our lives? I fully believe that God uses pain in our lives to strengthen us and prepare us for the plans he has for us and the ways he is going to use us. When we experience pain we have two options. We can either draw closer to God or turn away from him. When we allow our pain and trials and hardships to push us closer to God, our faith becomes stronger than ever before. Sometimes it takes being pushed to the breaking point for us to finally reach out to God and fully trust our entire lives to him. I think pain is a hard yet beautiful thing. Anyone who's been through something painful will tell you that though that time in their life was extremely hard, they would do it again because it shaped the person they are today. Pain isn't fun or easy, but it's necessary.

2. Do you believe God allows us to go through difficulties for a reason? I do believe that God allows us to go through difficulties for a reason. Our lives as Christians aren't supposed to be smooth, easy paths; if they are, then something's not right. As Christians we aren't promised a picture-perfect storybook life. We are promised hardships and trials, but with those hardships and trials we are promised Jesus Christ. Difficulties and hardships make us into better people. The image of iron sharpening iron is often used to describe this: just as a sword is held in the fire and then sharpened against another blade of iron in order to be made sharper and stronger, so we must go through the fire and be pushed across blades of iron to become the people God meant for us to be. Our lives aren't supposed to be easy; they're supposed to be hard. But through those hardships we have hope and joy in Jesus Christ.

3. What would you say to a kid who is experiencing pain and wondering where God is right now? As a young adult and teenager I went through some hard times when I truly questioned God and chose to back away from him. I wondered where he was and why he was allowing me to go through those things. Those times really sucked and were far from easy, but looking back at them now I can see how they shaped me into the person I am today. I needed to pull away from God and question him to truly make my faith my own and understand what it means to be a real follower of Jesus Christ. God was with me throughout those hardships and extremely painful times, and he was guiding me through a rocky path. Though I didn't always feel his presence or think he cared, I know he was constantly working in my life and waiting for me to return to him. No matter what we go through God is always there, and we have to choose to see him. He is holding out his arms, willing us to run into them, but sometimes our own stubborn and defiant nature keeps us from him. I would tell kids who are experiencing pain and an absence of God that he is waiting right in front of them with open arms and that they just need to make the choice to push forward into his embrace.

Practice
GENEROSITY

- Look for ways to become a part of other people's stories—for example, donate items to a friend's garage sale or bake sale fund-raiser. The more stories we become a part of the more we increase our impact as a family and the more we rejoice when others succeed.

- Time is often more precious than money. We teach our family an important lesson when they see us being generous with our time by volunteering at local non-profits, reading with our kids, or showing up in the lives of friends in need. Doing so is a huge indicator of where our hearts are.

10

Storing Our Treasures in Heaven

Joy is the serious business of Heaven.

C. S. Lewis

"Tell me about the kid who won everything tonight."

Jon-Avery looked at me and we both knew exactly whom I was talking about.

We were driving home from his eighth-grade public school awards assembly. He was still wearing his honor roll medal around his neck, but it didn't hide the slight slump of his shoulders. I asked the question because I could tell he needed to talk about what just happened.

I looked straight ahead and tried not to notice the slight quiver in his voice as he told me about the popular, highly decorated student who was also the very same person who had bullied one of Jon-Avery's friends all year long.

"I just don't understand, Mom. Why would that kid win Student of the Year when he's been so mean? It's just not fair," Jon-Avery said.

It wasn't the first conversation we'd had about the kid, but it was the first time I put a name with a face. When my son's name wasn't called as Student of the Year, I was honestly surprised. Not because he was the best at everything but because he had a heart of gold, and I figured others had noticed too.

I guess you'd have to know my son (and maybe from the previous chapters you feel like you do a little) to understand the kind of kid he is. He isn't perfect, but he is good. He's the kind of kid who doesn't go to a party hosted by a group of popular kids because they are the same ones who bullied his friend. He politely turned them down and instead invited over the boy who'd been excluded.

We don't give rewards for awards in our house. We definitely acknowledge achievements, but they aren't a goal. We've been saying "Do your best" for as long as I can remember. If your best is a big fat C, it's okay. Occasionally, it's my kids who walk across the stage decorated with awards, but more often they are in the middle of the pack.

I got a glimpse into what teachers and award-givers can't always see: my son had come behind one bent on popularity and achievement and quietly encouraged one left reeling in his wake.

We are raising kids in the age of awards—it's the trophy generation. Recently I attended an end-of-the-year elementary awards ceremony at which hundreds of names were called out. Every child received an award. I think awarding excellence is great because it encourages more excellence. But it gets tricky when we award everyone for participating so no one will feel left out. What are we encouraging exactly? Show up and you win!

Of course, awards aren't new. When I was in high school the only award I cherished was the Rhinestone Jesus Napkin Award (which was really a way for my drama club to mock my faith in a funny way. It didn't embarrass me; I was proud they noticed). It felt more like a reward than an award.

Life isn't fair. As adults we understand that truth, but it's hard to watch our kids learn it. It's not an easy lesson to see some recognized and others overlooked. But doing the right thing is still the right thing, and I reminded my son on that drive home that earthly awards have nothing to do with heavenly rewards. There's a difference between the two.

I reminded Jon-Avery of our conversation about heaven from the week before. Normally when I think about eternity it's during a worship service or when I'm completely overwhelmed. And then it's more of a "take me out of here, Jesus" thought. Spiritual, I know.

"Mom, heaven just doesn't sound that awesome," he had said. At least he was honest.

I told him about the time his little sister Emerson cried every time we talked about heaven. It all started out innocently enough. She was about three or four years old, and we were saying bedtime prayers and still doing a memorized version of this childhood prayer: "Now I lay me down to sleep, I pray the Lord my soul to keep. Angels watch me through the night, until I wake with morning light. Amen." She was precocious and a master at delay tactics and asked what it meant. I fell for it and began a long theological conversation in which I ended up describing eternity and how we would all live with Jesus.

"But I don't want to live with Jesus, Mommy. I want to live with you and Daddy," she said with tears in her eyes.

"Oh, it's okay, honey. It won't be now. It's later. Now let's go to bed." I was trying to work my way out of the conversation.

"But how do we get to heaven?" she asked. She clearly wasn't done.

I knew I couldn't tell her about death, so I said, "We will meet Jesus in the air. He will be on a white horse," because that seemed way less confusing. Yeah, right.

Within five minutes she was crying real tears, and I might have accidentally promised her a pony in heaven just like Jesus has. Only she wanted hers to be pink. I let Terrell handle bedtime prayers for weeks after that night.

Jon-Avery and I talked about what we would be doing "up there" for aeons and aeons. We had been listening to the radio, and a song I loved came on. I turned it up and sang off key. He rolled his eyes. When it ended I said, "I can't wait to sing that song for eternity." Based on his earlier comment, I think he imagined we would literally be singing the same song for a thousand years, and it left him with more questions than answers.

I assured him heaven wouldn't be what pop culture indicated. We wouldn't wear halos and feathered wings, strum harps, float on clouds, and sing all day and all night. At the time, I was in the middle of reading *The Treasure Principle* by Randy Alcorn, and I told him some of the things I'd learned about living in eternity with Jesus. I explained that we will work and will love our jobs. We will be filled with joy and eternal pleasure, and we will worship. We will also be rewarded for how we lived on earth. We talked about how everything we do here affects us in the afterlife—the good and bad choices we make.

I had underlined and earmarked pages in the book as a reminder for me, but in that moment I knew that this was something I had to also teach my kids. Alcorn writes:

John Bunyan wrote *Pilgrim's Progress* in an English prison. He said: "Whatever good thing you do for Him, if done according to the Word, is laid up for you as treasure in chests and coffers, to be brought out to be rewarded before both men and angels, to your eternal comfort."

Is this a biblical concept? Absolutely. Paul spoke about the Philippians' financial giving and explained, "Not that I am looking for a gift, but I am looking for what may be credited to your account" (Philippians 4:17). God keeps an account open for us in heaven, and every gift given for His glory is a deposit in that account. Not only God, not only others, but *we* are the eternal beneficiaries of our giving. (Have you been making regular deposits?)

But isn't it wrong to be motivated by reward? No, it isn't. If it were wrong, Christ wouldn't offer it to us as a motivation. Reward is His idea, not ours.

Our instinct is to give to those who will give us something in return. But Jesus told us to give to "the poor, the crippled, the lame, the blind. . . . Although they cannot repay you, you will be repaid at the resurrection of the righteous" (Luke 14:12–14). If we give to those who can't reward us, Christ guarantees He will personally reward us in heaven.

Giving is a giant lever positioned on the fulcrum of this world, allowing us to move mountains in the next world. Because we give, eternity will be different—for others and for us.[1]

I wish I could see how much "giving credit" I've got stored—it might just motivate me to do more. But just because I can't access my heavenly account doesn't mean it's not there. I love that Jesus is keeping track of it. One of my favorite passages has always been Matthew 6:19–20: "Do not store up for yourselves treasures on earth, where moths and vermin destroy, and where thieves break in and steal. But store up for yourselves treasures in heaven, where moths and vermin do not destroy, and where thieves do not break in and steal" (NIV). But what does this mean? Randy Alcorn says:

> It is by serving God and others that we store up heavenly treasures. Everyone gains. No one loses. . . . He who lays up treasures on earth spends his life backing away from his treasures. To him, death is loss. He who lays up treasures in heaven looks forward to eternity; he's moving daily toward his treasures. To him, death is gain. He who spends his life moving away from his treasures has reason to despair. He who spends his life moving toward his treasures has reason to rejoice.[2]

I explained this to Jon-Avery. "Son, it's a completely counter-cultural way to do math, but it adds up because God is keeping the record. He is taking note of who you are and what you do and how kind you are to people. He is recording it all, and it's been counted as treasures in heaven. It might not land you Student of the Year here on earth, but it will matter in eternity." This kind of accounting is hard to explain to our kids, but we can bank on the truth of it.

I wanted to know more about heaven to be better able to answer my kids' questions and began reading *Heaven*, also by Randy Alcorn. He says:

> Every kingdom work, whether publicly performed or privately endeavored, partakes of the kingdom's imperishable character. Every honest intention, every stumbling word of witness, every resistance of temptation, every motion of repentance, every gesture of concern, every routine engagement, every motion of worship, every struggle towards obedience, every mumbled prayer, everything, literally, which flows out of our faith-relationship with the Ever-Living One, will find

154

its place in the ever-living heavenly order which will dawn at his coming.[3]

Isn't that stunning? So, yes, trying counts!

A new friend got me to think about treasure in a completely new way. Over lunch we talked about faith, the church, and perspective, and she asked, "If you could tell the church anything, what would it be?"

Without having to think, I knew my answer. "I would tell the church that we can continue to compete with the world, constantly trying to better our lifestyles with bigger and better cars, houses, and so on, or we can change lives."

Our conversation made me think about something I'd read in the book of James. I pulled out my Bible and read the following:

> Look here, you rich people: Weep and groan with anguish because of all the terrible troubles ahead of you. Your wealth is rotting away, and your fine clothes are moth-eaten rags. Your gold and silver are corroded. The very wealth you were counting on will eat away your flesh like fire. This corroded treasure you have hoarded will testify against you on the day of judgment.
>
> For listen! Hear the cries of the field workers whom you have cheated of their pay. The wages you held back cry out against you. The cries of those who harvest your fields have reached the ears of the LORD of Heaven's Armies. You have spent your years on earth in luxury, satisfying your every desire. You have fattened yourselves for the day of slaughter. You have condemned and killed innocent people, who do not resist you. (James 5:1–6 NLT)

I studied it and reread it several times, and these words from *An Exposition of the Bible* gave me much to think about:

They imagined themselves to be rich; they were really most poor and most miserable. So sure is the doom that is coming upon them, that in prophetical style St. James begins to speak of it as already here; like a seer, he has it all before his eyes. "Your riches are corrupted, and your garments are moth-eaten. Your gold and your silver are rusted." We have here three kinds of possessions indicated. First, stores of various kinds of goods. These are "corrupted"; they have become rotten and worthless. Secondly, rich garments, which in the East are often a very considerable portion of a wealthy man's possessions. They have been stored up so jealously and selfishly that insects have preyed upon them and ruined them. And thirdly, precious metals. These have become tarnished and rusted, through not having been put to any rational use. Everywhere their avarice has been not only sin, but folly. It has failed of its sinful object. The unrighteous hoarding has tended not to wealth, but to ruin. And thus the rust of their treasures becomes "a testimony against them." In the ruin of their property their own ruin is portrayed; and just as corruption, and the moths, and the rust consume their goods, so shall the fire of God's judgment consume the owners and abusers of them. They have reserved all this store for their selfish enjoyment, but God has reserved them for His righteous anger.[4]

I immediately thought of Matthew 6:19–20, where we are urged to store up treasures in heaven and not on earth to prevent these same calamities. In other words, not only should we store up treasures in heaven by how we serve others and give to people in need—basically by how we live—but also if we choose to store our treasures on earth they will be the only reward we get.

We were created for heaven. We are eternal beings; this world will never truly satisfy us. We try too hard to quench the hunger for more with the things of this world, but the more we get the emptier we feel. I know because that's how I spent many years of my life. Once I began storing my treasures in heaven instead of spending them on myself, I started longing for heaven more. I finally understood Colossians 3:1–2, which commands: "Set your hearts on things above, where Christ is, seated at the right hand of God. Set your minds on things above, not on earthly things" (NIV). We are supposed to long for heaven.

I truly believe these words from Randy Alcorn:

> Nothing is more often misdiagnosed than our homesickness for Heaven. We think that what we want is sex, drugs, alcohol, a new job, a raise, a doctorate, a spouse, a large-screen television, a new car, a cabin in the woods, a condo in Hawaii. What we really want is the person we were made for, Jesus, and the place we were made for, Heaven. Nothing less can satisfy us.[5]

I think this is why we have pain and suffering here on earth. It makes us long for the place where neither of those will exist. We all bear our own kind of hardships in this life. Terrell and I have chosen to expose our kids to the pain and suffering of the world, not to harm them but to help them. The last thing we want to do is raise kids who can see only their own suffering. When we show them the pain of others, we not only give them perspective but also teach them compassion. And we raise kids who change the world.

Think about it. It's when we are in pain that we discover God is the only true source of our contentment. It's up to us as parents to redirect and remind our children that this world—with all its must-haves—will never satisfy. Abigail Van Buren, better

157

known as "Dear Abby," gave this practical advice to parents: "If you want your children to turn out well, spend twice as much time with them, and half as much money."[6]

In an article on heaven in *Thriving Family* from Focus on the Family, Randy Alcorn suggests we teach our kids these five truths about heaven:

1. *Heaven won't be boring.* God isn't boring and neither is heaven. God has a limitless imagination.

2. *Heaven is not our default destination.* There are two roads, but only one path leads to heaven—choosing Jesus. We need to talk to our kids about heaven and hell. Randy says, "The most loving thing we can do for our families is to clearly explain the road that leads to destruction—and the road that leads to life."

3. *Heaven is a real, physical place.* "My Father's house has many rooms. . . . I am going there to prepare a place for you" (John 14:2 NIV).

4. *Heaven is the completion of our redemption.* God has had a plan since creation. Man messed up the plan in the Garden of Eden, and God sent Jesus to redeem us. Heaven is both the end and the new beginning.

5. *Heaven inspires our faith.* Heaven gives us something to hope for and reminds us that God will redeem everything.[7]

As I drove Jon-Avery through Chick-fil-A for a sweet tea (my kind of reward) on the way home from his awards ceremony, I reminded him of our earlier conversation about heaven. "What you're doing now, how you're living and loving and leading, the way you seek out the kid left out and left behind—these are worth a reward. The medal kind given out tonight will rust and end up in a box in the attic, but the kind you're storing up in heaven—this kind will last forever."

I also reminded him that just because our culture doesn't always value the good guys who are quietly making the right decisions, rooting for the underdog, loving and serving the least of these, that doesn't mean these acts are not being recorded.

Someone is taking account. I gave him a little nudge and said, "One day, instead of gold around our neck it will be under our feet." He rolled his eyes, but he was also sitting up straighter.

I think my son was beginning to understand the truth behind why we serve others, why we love and give away our time, our money, our friendship—what we have:

Our giving is a reflexive response to the grace of God in our lives. It doesn't come out of our altruism or philanthropy—it comes out of the transforming work of Christ in us. This grace is the action; our giving is the reaction. We give because He first gave to us. The greatest passage on giving in all Scripture ends not with "Congratulations for your generosity," but "Thanks be to God for his indescribable gift!" (2 Cor. 9:15). We give because we have received, and when we do we store up treasures in Heaven that we will enjoy for eternity.[8]

Start WORLD-CHANGING CONVERSATIONS *with Your Kids*

I asked my son, Jon-Avery, to answer the following questions. I hope they lead to good conversations with your kids.

1. Who do you long to meet one day? I think that out of everyone I could meet, I have to go with the very "Christian" answer. I want to meet Jesus. I want to be in his arms and know one day that I did good, that I ran my race with perseverance and didn't give up. I know that can sound cliché, but everything else will pale in comparison to him because everything good and perfect comes from him. He is the purpose for my life, the only thing that will ever satisfy, and when we are in heaven he will satisfy us for the rest of eternity.

2. Do you ever think about meeting God? Honestly, I have thought about the idea of meeting God, but the actual act of meeting my Creator, my Savior, my Father in person . . . it's a little daunting. The whole idea of eternity and a place where we will spend it has always scared me, but I have found peace with it. I know that I will never understand all of it, and I have realized that trying to will just leave me with more doubts and questions I cannot answer. I have learned to give those doubts to God, ask him for peace, and trust in what he does tell me about heaven. I know it will be good, and I know I will see him in person, but I have already met God. He is my Father, and I am in relationship with him every day.

That is why I am able to live my life in anticipation of what is to come when I return home to God.

3. What do you think heaven will be like? I don't know if words can describe it, but I think I know what it will feel like. Often when I come to God in worship, I am overcome with gratitude, with thanksgiving for what he has done, overwhelmed with all the needs he has met. I am able to truly let go of my burdens and give them to God and feel close to him. That feeling of closeness and communion with God is what I think heaven will be like. I imagine that feeling will be amplified and a part of everything we will do. We may not be singing a song to God for all eternity, but I think that we will be in a constant state of worship and closeness to him.

Practice
GENEROSITY

- Pack a generous lunch by including an extra snack for your child to share. Talk to them about giving and how it feels to share what they have with others.

- Be generous with your apologies. Sometimes modeling the behavior we want is the best way to see it in our kids. Saying "I'm sorry" when we've lost our temper or hurt our kids' feelings is a good way to show generosity to them.

11

A Family Soul-Care Plan

> If you want to change the world,
> go home and love your family.
>
> Mother Teresa

I ran into a friend at the library where I was typing out the words to this chapter. She peeked at my computer over my shoulder and said, "Oh, you're working on your new book? What's it about?"

"Um . . ." You'd think I'd have my elevator pitch down, and it would be an easy question. "Generosity."

"Hmm . . . So like a book on giving back?" she asked.

"No, it's a book about *giving it all*," I answered.

Yeah, I'm not so sure she added it to her reading list.

When we read through the Gospels that chronicle the life of Jesus, we can come to only one conclusion: Jesus gave everything.

What did it cost Jesus? *Everything.*

What should it cost us? *Everything.*

Jesus doesn't ask us to just give back—he asks us to give it all.

It's as hard to type these words as it is to read them. We skirt our way around this truth in our faith culture. Sure, we give back, but Jesus says, "No, give it all."

It's not sexy or cute or fun. Seriously, what happens when we give it all to him? We fear we will have nothing left—no money, time, resources, or dreams.

But as strange as it sounds, this is the kingdom formula to having it all. In his book *Radical*, David Platt says, "We are settling for a Christianity that revolves around catering to ourselves when the central message of Christianity is actually about abandoning ourselves."[1]

There's nothing confusing or unclear about Jesus's words to his disciples as he prepared for the cross: "Whoever wants to be my disciple must deny themselves and take up their cross daily and follow me. For whoever wants to save their life will lose it, but whoever loses their life for me will save it" (Luke 9:23–24 NIV).

This "deny yourself and follow me" road isn't easy. There aren't guarantees of safety and security. As a matter of fact, there are many risks along the way. I want to explore two of them with you.

First, *giving it all means we empty ourselves*. But if we aren't consistently taking time to refill and recharge, we find rather quickly that we have nothing left to give.

In the middle of writing this chapter, I had to stop and take a long break. Somewhere in the process of getting these thoughts on paper, I discovered that I wasn't just weary and tired from a hectic season. I was completely empty. Again.

I haven't always taken good care of my soul.

The best way to know you need soul care is when it feels too late to get it. I didn't even know the term *soul care* until

October 2015 when I got an unexpected email from someone I'd never heard of inviting me to join her and a handful of other nonprofit leaders at an all-expenses-paid weekend at the Ritz Carlton in Vail, Colorado. Um, excuse me? I sort of dismissed it with the other robocallers who want to give me money. But Brandi, the gal on the other end of the computer, was persistent.

I learned that SoulCare Retreats was legitimate, and after talking to a couple of women who had benefited from the relaxing weekend—where you're pampered and loved and given space to let God renew you—I began to consider it. Terrell would have put me on the next plane out of town because those closest to us see burnout long before we are going up in flames. The last trip he talked me into was my first trip to Kenya in 2010, so I was both excited and terrified. I said yes.

I read the agenda for the retreat while in my car waiting in line to pick up my youngest from school. A lump formed in my throat as I read the words *rest, renewal, unscheduled time to relax, no agenda*, and by the time I got to *a quiet time to care for your soul* I was undone. I sat in my dirty minivan and cried until I couldn't breathe.

For months I had been feeling anxious and more overwhelmed than normal, and those feelings were preceded by years of carrying a crushing burden. My life had become one meeting after another, answering emails all hours of the day, staying up late to complete writing assignments, and filling my days at the Mercy House warehouse. I had become a master multitasker, juggling motherhood, marriage, and ministry, but even pro jugglers drop balls.

I was so tired. I was weary in well doing. I've never been good at resting, and I realized I stink at caring for my soul. I was functioning on fumes, and I felt panic every time I looked at my list of things to do.

I began reading passages of Scripture about Jesus removing himself for solitude, finding secluded places of prayer, and even napping on a boat in a storm. It dawned on me that my refusal to stop and rest to renew my soul wasn't strength; it was weakness. It was pride.

I've heard it said that keeping the Sabbath is experiencing freedom. I didn't really understand this until I admitted how hard it was for me to stop working and actually rest. In Deuteronomy 5 we read: "Observe the Sabbath day by keeping it holy. . . . Remember that you were slaves in Egypt and that the LORD your God brought you out of there with a mighty hand and an outstretched arm" (vv. 12, 15 NIV). About Sabbath rest Tim Keller says:

> In the Bible, Sabbath rest means to cease regularly from and to enjoy the results of your work. . . . Sabbath is about more than external rest of the body; it is about inner rest of the soul. We need rest from the anxiety and strain of our overwork, which is really an attempt to justify ourselves—to gain the money or the status or the reputation we think we have to have.[2]

At some point I believed the very dangerous lie that all the things I was involved in—family, work, ministry—functioned only because of me. But I recommitted to being more like Jesus, and if he needed to retreat occasionally, how much more did I need to. Once I gave in to rest, I saw how desperately I needed it as a wife, mother, and leader. When I first walked into my gorgeous room in Vail in October of 2015 and saw the spectacular snowy mountain view, I burst into tears. I lay down on the bed and sobbed until I couldn't cry anymore. I was treated like royalty with presents and massages and amazing food. I spent hours alone. I read and prayed. I took long bubble baths, and I learned to be still again. I enjoyed every second.

A few months later, my family welcomed into our home Maureen, our Kenyan director who leads the maternity homes we support, and her family for a twenty-seven-day stay. It's an annual visit we look forward to, but it's not always easy. Inviting guests from the third world into our first world always breaks me in a new way. It's impossible not to see how much wealth we have through the fresh eyes of people who have so much less.

We had a hectic schedule of speaking and fund-raising. In a three-month time frame we hosted our Annual Gala, moved our nonprofit into a warehouse five times the size, opened our first fair-trade retail store, and hosted a gathering of nonprofit leaders—most of which we did while having houseguests for a month. It was a demanding and exhausting season, but I watched my family come together and serve. Our kids shared their parents and the demands on our time. Jon-Avery gladly offered his room for the long visit and slept on the couch. Madison helped prepare meals, and Emerson was a huge blessing each time she played with and occupied Amaziah, their young son. It was a time that stretched us in every way—financially (extra mouths to feed and the opportunity to spoil our friends), physically (demanding schedule), and emotionally (listening to hard stories, planning, and so on).

Terrell and I modeled loving God and loving others to our children. But we also showed them how to overburden a family, put strain on a marriage, and take a giant step toward burnout. What we were doing during this time sounds good on paper, but there were hard days, meltdowns, and angry moments. During one particularly tough day I was arguing with my kids because

I needed more of their help during the two-week period that Maureen and I had twelve speaking engagements. Madison said, "Sometimes I feel like everything is about Mercy House."

Her words felt like a slap. Not in a disrespectful way but in a wake-up-call way. And she was right. Some days it did feel that way. Her words were exactly what I needed to remember the important balance we were lacking. I remembered my time in Colorado, and I realized my family needed soul care as much as I had needed it months before. We had a family meeting that night and circled a date on our calendar a week away to love our family well so that we could love the world well. One is entirely dependent on the other.

Sometimes our children speak truth more than anyone else, but we may have to listen through their tears or screams. Some of my most painful lessons of motherhood have been when my kids begged me to rest. It sounded like "Lay with me, Mom," or it looked like a demanding teenager who was desperately trying to get my attention.

Colorado had become the place for our family to rest, renew, and even heal. (We tend to mess up our kids on this parenting journey no matter how hard we try not to.) Our friends continued to offer us their home as often as we could get away. We had some needed conversations, made some apologies, and took some steps closer to each other. Sometimes we don't realize how far we are from one another until we pause our busy lives and make a conscious effort to reconnect.

But soul care isn't a biannual retreat or a cabin in Colorado. It's drinking daily from the source of life; we cannot lead our families to fullness if we are bone dry. One of our volunteers at Mercy House explained it this way, "We open our hands to what God gives us. It could be time or money or both. We keep one hand open so we can share what we have with others and the other hand open so God can keep filling it." At the time I was in the middle of this self-imposed book-writing break because I was desperately empty. As she stood in the middle of our warehouse with her palms open, I saw that I had one hand open to share what God had given, but the other hand wasn't open to receive more. It was busy working.

A second risk along the "deny yourself and follow me" road is this: *giving it all doesn't mean we work harder.*

At Mercy House, 2017 started off with more stress than I thought possible due to staff changes, unprecedented growth, and a pressing burden to maintain all we had begun to empower women globally. It was also the first year we had transitioned our two teens out of public school to an online high school at their request, and everything was tougher than we thought it would be. In May of that year I had one of my children at our dear pediatrician's office and described their symptoms as moody, exhausted, and angry. The doctor asked several questions, including, "When did this begin?" I thought about it and said, "Well, I guess after we got back from Kenya in March." She has been doctoring my kids since they were toddlers and knows all about Mercy House. She's given them yellow-fever shots and malaria medicine to protect them. "Kristen, I think maybe your kids are just trying to process what they experienced." I started crying, and that visit turned out to be a little family-therapy session. We had cared for our physical bodies, but our souls were weary. Our family circled the first week of June, the first week of summer, on our calendars, as a finish line of sorts or at least as a break to come up for air. More than once I looked at that circled date and mentally counted down the days until we could take that first deep, long breath of Colorado air.

Two weeks before our summer trip and after battling a bad cold, I completed my last speaking event of the school year. When I arrived home at midnight and realized we had company coming the next day, I checked the calendar again and thought, *I can do this*. The kids were on fumes too, and I reminded them the finish line was in sight.

Then one week before our trip our family was at the park across the street from our house with our houseguests. Jon-Avery had ridden his skateboard to the park, and on impulse Terrell got on it and rode off down the street with our dog jogging beside him.

Ten minutes later a neighbor was driving down the street toward the park yelling my name. My blood ran cold when I saw my husband crumpled in the seat next to him. "You need to take your husband to the hospital now," the neighbor said. After a night in the emergency room, doctors confirmed what we feared: Terrell had crushed his ankle and would need surgery to rebuild it.

The next morning the surgeon put my husband on complete bed rest for the next ten days to try to reduce the swelling so that when he performed the surgery he would be able to close the incisions in his leg. I cried when the doctor left the room because I realized we would have to cancel our Colorado vacation.

Sometimes when you try to take that desperately needed deep breath, you find there's no air in your lungs. That's exactly how our family felt—like the breath had been kicked out of us. I thought there was nothing more our family needed than cool mountain air. God thought differently. Our lives slowed to almost a complete stop while we waited for that surgery and for weeks afterward. We didn't leave our house for days and days. People brought us meals for weeks. While my husband mended,

God did something unexpected in our hearts. He showed our family that rest comes in many ways and that sometimes soul care looks completely different than we think it should. I had time to think and pray and be still. There weren't majestic mountains (unless you count laundry piles) or rocky mountain springs (unless you count my clean commodes), but God was there. He has a way of giving us what we need.

That's not to say it was the summer we hoped for—there were plenty of tears and pouting and complaining (and that was just me). Early on I told Terrell, "Maybe God has a lesson for us to learn in all this." I think we learned much about ourselves during this time. I discovered afresh how much my husband does for our family on a daily basis. He serves us without complaint, and we had grown accustomed to it. With him on bed rest for weeks, all the things he normally did either didn't get done or were done by the kids and me. We tried to remember to put out the trash, mow the lawn, pay the bills, and so on. I was also reminded how much he helps me. More than once I started to ask him to bring me something, put our youngest to bed, or run an errand before I remembered that he couldn't. And Terrell felt terrible. I think we both discovered we had too much pride. It was hard on Terrell not to be able to do those things that always came naturally to him. It was hard for me to accept help from others.

This season became a time to receive. Giving didn't always come naturally for my family, but once we started, it became addictive. Receiving, on the other hand, is much harder. It's humbling to let other people feed your family. It's difficult to let friends grocery shop for you, pick up your kids, walk your dog, bring in your trash, mow your yard—you name it. But nothing will make you feel more loved.

171

One night when a friend dropped off a meal she'd spent hours preparing, she hugged my neck and whispered, "Keep going, girl." It reminded me of the last time I was in Colorado.

I was actually on my way home from a SoulCare Retreat reunion of more than forty nonprofit leaders, and I had a forty-five-minute layover in the Denver airport before my flight home. It wasn't a lot of time, but sometimes a little is all you need. The night before as I repacked my suitcase to head home, one of our very first and longest Mercy House donors messaged me and asked if she and her kids could meet me at the airport "for just a minute to encourage you."

I never pass up encouragement so I sent her the time and terminal. We found each other in a sea of travelers, and her adorable little kids gave me big hugs like we were long-lost friends. We settled down at a nearby table at the airport Burger King, and they handed me a greeting card, a Chick-fil-A gift card, a package of homemade oatmeal chocolate chip cookies (my favorite), and a beautiful paper crown. Just because, of course.

While the kids shared a soda, I caught up with an online-turned-real-life friend. I had just spent three days at a SoulCare Retreat with a room full of world changers who were so raw and real and vulnerable that I felt at home standing in front of them, sobbing uncontrollably, and letting them into a painful parenting place I haven't shared with many. (Oh yes, we all have them. That kid who challenges, pushes, frustrates, discourages you. You know the one. Sometimes we just need to tell someone so they can remind us that parenting is hard and we aren't alone.)

So when my airport visitor asked me how I was doing—really doing—I told her.

I told her life was good and life was hard. That this yes might just kill me, but I would die happy and satisfied. Sometimes when people ask, they really want to know.

My layover time was ticking and my friend called her kiddos over and asked, "Would you like to ask Mrs. Welch your questions now?" She turned to me and said, "Mercy House is a part of our lives. My kids have grown up praying for you."

I got a giant lump in my throat.

They asked about the water well we dug in Kenya and about the maternity home and then this question, "Have you ever been persecuted?" They paused. "Like has anyone ever thrown rocks at you?"

Not real ones, I thought. But I told them about some of our Fair Trade Friday groups in India who were facing violence and opposition for their faith, and I asked these littlest supporters to pray for them.

I looked at my watch; it was time to go. They walked me to the escalator, and we took some pictures. They hugged me again, and I grabbed my bags, my paper crown, and the unopened card and hurried toward security.

Once I settled into my seat on the plane I took a deep breath and felt a surge of exhausted relief to be heading home again to my family. I opened the card my friend had given me and the first words were "Keep going, girl. . . ."

In row 26 I ate an oatmeal chocolate chip cookie and I cried. Because that was exactly what I needed to hear.

I'm really bad at taking care of myself. And sometimes when you put off caring for yourself it takes time to catch up. That's what I'm doing. I'm also trying not to give up. Maybe you need to hear these words too. Keep going, girl . . .

Keep going when it gets hard.

Keep going when it stays hard.

Keep going when you really want to give up.

Keep going when you're afraid and everyone thinks you're brave.

Keep going when you're too tired to stand.

Keep going when where you're going is here instead of there.

I love my job. I love to work. I'm not sure when it happened but at some point work became easier than rest. I have a hard time relaxing and being still. When I was forced to stop I discovered that some of my work was really a need to prove myself, as if all I do depended on me rather than God. No, it wasn't the summer we wanted, but I really think it became the summer we needed. It was the summer God taught our weary family to rest in the gospel and the summer God reminded us that he was satisfied with us. Tim Keller says:

> Most of us work and work trying to prove ourselves, to convince God, others, and ourselves that we're good people. That work is never over unless we rest in the gospel. At the end of His great act of creation the Lord said, "It is finished," and He could rest. On the cross at the end of His great act of redemption Jesus said, "It is finished" and we can rest. On the cross Jesus was saying of the work underneath your work—the thing that makes you truly weary, this need to prove yourself because who you are and what you do are never good enough—that it is finished. He has lived the life you should have lived, He has died the death you should have died. If you rely on Jesus's finished work, you know that God is satisfied with you. You can be satisfied with life.[3]

When Jesus said, "It is finished," he was literally telling us, "You're approved. No more trying to prove yourself; you are covered in my blood. You can't live up to my Father's standard because you are fallen and sinful, but I can. I did. I sacrificed. And now I cover you. You're approved."

I'm taking my own advice. I started going to regular counseling sessions so I can process the burden I carry, the exhaustion in my soul, and the beauty and heartbreak of giving my all. I started taking a regular day off to rest. And we decided to take two weeks off at the end of that difficult summer. Rest isn't always sleeping; it's sometimes being still.

Here are five things we can teach our kids about soul care if we slow down long enough to learn these lessons ourselves:

1. Be vulnerable with people who want to know how you're really doing.
2. Insist on time alone. And time together with your family alone. You need it more than you think you do.
3. Retreat to a quiet place and listen to God. He always says something, even if it's "be still."
4. Surround yourself with a community of broken people who share a common journey (for example, adoption, leadership, teenagers, toddlers).
5. Wear a crown and celebrate. Sometimes we have to look behind us to see how far we've come. And whatever you do, just keep going.

It's easy to lose ourselves in caring for others. Parents, we can only give away what we possess ourselves. Schedule some time to care for yourselves so you can care for your families.

And let God renew your soul.

Start
WORLD-CHANGING
CONVERSATIONS
with Your Kids

I asked my husband, Terrell, to answer the following questions for this chapter. I hope they lead to good conversations with your family.

1. Why is rest important? I think when we rest we remind ourselves that we are fragile and finite. So often we try to be completely self-sufficient and do things all on our own. Stopping to rest acknowledges that God is sovereign and that he expects us to recharge. Resting in the Bible is almost always accompanied with spending personal time with God. Remember the Sabbath and keep it holy. I have always believed that the biggest issue in every Christian's life is trust. Either we trust that God knows what is best for us, or we believe that we know better than God what is best for us. When we rest, it's like a silent nod to God: "Lord, I can't do this on my own strength. I put my trust in you, and I take time to renew my mind and spirit." Billions of people around the world plug in their cell phones every night. We wouldn't dream of walking around with a cell phone that has a dead battery. It becomes a useless paperweight in our pocket—no apps, no texts, no phone calls, not even 911. Our body, soul, and spirit are essentially the same. If we have not devoted quality time to rest and sleep then our battery is dead. If our battery is dead then we're useless to ourselves, our family, and the kingdom.

Matthew 11:28–30 sums up well the idea of rest and trust: "Are you tired? Worn out? Burned out on religion? Come to me. Get away with me and you'll recover your life. I'll show you how to take a real rest. Walk with me and work with me—watch how I do it. Learn the unforced rhythms of grace. I won't lay anything heavy or ill-fitting on you. Keep company with me and you'll learn to live freely and lightly."

2. What do you think God wants us to learn from times of "forced stillness"?
I think one of the biggest lessons that I've learned is that I have neglected rest and spending time with God. My battery was definitely run down, and I was trusting in myself. We quote Proverbs 3:5–6 so often that I wonder if we really understand the meaning. "Trust in the Lord"—is my trust in God or in myself? "With all your heart"—this is all or nothing. As Yoda says to Luke Skywalker, "Do or do not. There is no try." God is not satisfied with a part of us. It's all or nothing. "Do not lean on your own understanding"—thinking we know what is best always leads us down the wrong path. "In all your ways acknowledge him"—he wants everything. Lord, my family is yours. My spouse is yours. My secrets are known to you. When we have done all that the verse says, "He will direct your paths." I have to trust God. I don't know what the future holds. It could be a broken leg or it could be cancer. If I trust God, it doesn't matter. My life is lived for the purpose of other people seeing his glory. I've also come to realize that I take a lot of pride in being fiercely independent when it comes to everyday life. This injury taught me not only to trust in God but also to rely on others and be thankful when they serve me.

177

3. How can you teach your kids to be still and get alone time with God? We have to teach our kids that God can speak to us through his Word and through prayer when we are alone with him. Next we practice with them. Read the Word, pray together, and sit in silence. A few minutes later ask them if they learned anything from the Scripture or if they felt as though God spoke to them. If we make this normal it will be. Lastly, we have to model it. I remember many times getting up for school to find my dad with a cup of coffee next to his recliner and the Bible open on his lap. One night very early in the morning, I heard my dad. I walked into the living room and saw him with his face buried in his hands crying out to God. This is what my kids need to see in me and what your kids need to see in you. I don't want to be ashamed to cry in front of my kids during worship at church or to have them discover me pouring out my heart to God. Real learning takes place by first modeling and then giving our kids a chance to put it into practice.

Practice
GENEROSITY

- Be generous to yourself. Get your family into the art of practicing soul care. Give everyone a journal and encourage them to write conversations to God.

- Create space for rest. Close your eyes, take deep breaths, and reflect on Scripture.

- Have regular family meetings (dinner is a great time) and ask your kids whom they would like to serve and/ or help. Sometimes we just need an invitation to share our thoughts.

12

The Answer

We Can Change Our Lifestyles,
or We Can Change a Life

But if anyone has the world's goods and sees
his brother in need, yet closes his heart against him,
how does God's love abide in him?

1 John 3:17 ESV

It turns out that when you decide to write a book on generosity God might just drop a large, unexpected amount of money in your lap. No kidding, that's exactly what happened.

I drive by my dream house on the way to work every day. During the spring when it was being built, Terrell and I impulsively stopped and looked in the windows. I told myself if we got caught peeking into the vacant house, we could convince people we were potential buyers and not creepers.

A contractor opened the front door with us standing on the porch. It was as awkward as it sounds, but he was happy to give us the grand tour and confirm that, yes, this was definitely our dream house and it could be ours for a small fortune. My husband and I had one or two what-if conversations. "What if we sold our house and what if we got a little higher house payment and what if we used the extra space to . . . and what if we . . ." and we talked about all the reasons and ways we could make this happen. We even dipped our toes into these murky waters and said to each other, "We are good people. We help others." Although we didn't say it out loud we might even have thought that maybe we deserve this blessing.

But in our hearts we knew the what-ifs would make our *we coulds* impossible. It is the *we coulds* that have made our lives such an adventure. We could sponsor another child. We could start a nonprofit and raise money to open maternity homes in Kenya. We could buy a kiln for an artisan group we work with at Fair Trade Friday. We could support our sweet friend and employee who wants to move to Thailand to serve her people. We could respond to a need immediately. We could . . .

Back in my own beautiful home, I gave myself a pep talk every now and then when I started to think about what I didn't have instead of what I did. My thoughts went like this: *Kristen, your house is beautiful and has plenty of room. Moving would be so much trouble. We've spent so much time and money on our backyard.*

But even the *we coulds* didn't stop me from noticing the for sale sign swinging in the wind as I slowed down to pass my dream house, and they didn't stop me from wondering what it would be like to sip coffee on the broad porch swing or cook in the modern farmhouse kitchen. Our kids overheard the small talk about a dream house and noticed every time we drove slowly by it and put two and two together. It didn't take long for it to become their dream house too. "Mom, drive by the house!" they would urge me on every trip home.

During spring break when that dream house was going up my family traveled back to Kenya. We visited the maternity homes, held miracle babies, took new fair-trade product ideas to artisan groups, and witnessed hope. It got us through the hopeless situations such as visiting with Agnes, a mom who told us her daughter got pregnant at fourteen.

"She was in the sixth grade," she tells us. She wasn't promiscuous or disobedient; she was desperate. I didn't ask what it was like to let your little girl sleep with old men for food because the tears rolling down her cheeks were answer enough.

Her pregnant daughter is now a young mom, rescued and thriving at the maternity home funded by Mercy House Global. Our family started the nonprofit more than seven years ago for survival prostitutes, those who prostitute for food and survival—for girls just like this daughter.

I sat in this mother's home with my fourteen-year-old next to me, and I could barely breathe.

This mom also told us how her son was still owned by a neighbor who lived down the littered road in the slum. He worked all day and most nights—not for money but for food. I wondered if she knew we called this slavery.

She told us how she boiled corn to sell to people on their way home from work and tried to provide for her seven children after her drunkard husband ran off, but month after month she came up short and had to make desperate decisions to keep her family fed. I didn't know what to say or what to do, but I knew we had to do something or her daughter and grandchild would never be able to come home.

I won't lie, as I scratched my crawling skin in the stifling heat and could still feel the glares of men staring down my daughters as we walked to her house, I couldn't wait to leave her home. I didn't feel brave at all and longed to return to my normal.

I closed my eyes and held back tears. This is 75 percent of the world's normal. It's a truth that's easy to ignore: a small percentage of us have enough of the world's resources to last a lifetime, while a large percentage of the world doesn't have enough for even one day.

Before we left the house I pulled out my phone to show her pictures I'd taken of her daughter and granddaughter at the maternity home the day before. She tenderly touched the screen and wiped her eyes; her pride was evident. Then I showed her a picture of me holding her granddaughter, and I could no longer stop the tears. You see, her granddaughter was named Kristen after me. Baby Kristen made Agnes and me family forever. I treasured the moment, and I think my family sitting around me did too.

We left her home and found a place to shake the bugs out of our clothes, and we cried over lunch with the heaviness of the world's normal. We already offered small-business and parenting training, but our small team—our kids included—racked our brains on how to take the next steps to provide new jobs and a central workspace for the desperate mothers we had visited that morning. We returned home, vowing to change their lives.

The entire time we were in Kenya we didn't think of our dream house once. I didn't think of the gorgeous wood-beam ceilings when I stood in a home without a roof. I didn't remember the massive front porch when I stepped over putrid raw sewage to enter a home in the slum. I didn't long for the perfect kitchen when I sat in home after home without running water.

Once we were back home, I decided to go a different way to work so as not to pass by the dream house. I no longer cared about it. My kids never mentioned it again either. I was reminded of this truth—this choice—that our culture and even the church and, yes, I don't like to think about: I can change my lifestyle, or I can change a life.

On a Saturday a few weeks after we got home we were doing yard work. The guys were mowing and weed whacking while the girls and I pulled weeds in the flower beds. I took a break to grab the mail. I opened the mailbox and pulled out a letter and some bills. I opened an envelope from my publisher and couldn't believe what I was holding. It was a very large, very unexpected royalty check. I let out a gasp and my family looked up from working. I waved it in the air and they came over. "Oh my goodness, oh my goodness!" I said.

"What is it?" my son and husband asked in unison.

I told them and Emerson said, "Momma, what are we going to do with that money?"

Before I could answer, these words flashed in my mind, *Is this a blessing or a test?* I knew the answer. "Honey, we are going to change lives with it."

We can keep changing our lifestyles with every raise and "blessing" that comes our way, or we can change a life. That's the hard truth in the daily choices we make. Yes, the truth hurts. I will tell you plainly, it is gutting me. I have met women in oppressive and pathetic situations who are hoping and praying we will make the right choice.

I can make my life better, more comfortable, and more convenient, or I can change another person's life so they can live another day. When we say it hard and clear like that, it almost makes it sound as if we are choosing between being selfish or selfless.

Right after that trip to Kenya, I stood in front of women at a church, and the words that had been thundering in my heart for weeks came out of my mouth. I was as shocked to hear them as those with dropped jaws staring back at me were. I'm still trying to sort out the thoughts and feelings in my heart, and some days I swing too far to one side or the other. But saying them aloud has made them seem only truer. We call ourselves a blessed people. America is blessed. We are a Christian nation, and God has blessed us with so many good things, pretty things. I have a nice car, a nice house; I am so blessed.

We get unexpected money in the mail and we say, "Oh, look, another blessing." But what if God gave it to us so we could bless someone else with it? What if instead of giving God the minimum we gave him the most? What if we aren't blessed at all? What if we have so much not because we are blessed but because we simply keep it ourselves? What if we have been given so much because we are supposed to give it away and not keep it? What if we are really just selfish? What if we are failing instead of succeeding?

We can change our lifestyles, or we can change lives.

Often when we change our lifestyles we saddle ourselves with debt and payments and we couldn't change a life—ours included—even if we wanted to. When we have so much stuff, always trading in and up for bigger and better, we don't feel less burdened; we feel only more tethered to this earth. I can say it because I have lived it—so heavy with stuff that it nearly choked me to death.

I cannot get Mother Teresa's words out of my head, "When a poor person dies of hunger, it has not happened because God did not take care of him or her. It has happened because neither you nor I wanted to give that person what he or she needed."[1]

What if we took Richard Stearns's version of Scripture to heart:

> For I was hungry, while you had all you needed. I was thirsty, but you drank bottled water. I was a stranger, and you wanted me deported. I needed clothes, but you needed more clothes. I was sick, and you pointed out the behaviors that led to my sickness. I was in prison, and you said I was getting what I deserved.[2]

We must consider this question asked by David Platt: "If our lives do not reflect radical compassion for the poor, there is reason to wonder if Christ is really in us at all."[3] What if we changed the way we live so that other people could live? What if we were changed in the process? What if we believed these words: "By this we know love, that he laid down his life for us, and we ought to lay down our lives for the brothers. But if anyone has the world's goods and sees his brother in need, yet closes his heart against him, how does God's love abide in him?" (1 John 3:16–17 ESV). God help us to see the truth, even when it hurts. We either believe this truth, or we don't.

One night after that trip, as summer was in full swing, Madison sat down heavily on the couch next to me. I could tell she wanted to talk, so I closed my laptop, turned toward her, and waited. I refused to fill the silence with words, and eventually she started talking. (Sometimes this simple action is all we need to take to get our kids to open up.) "Mom, I just feel different from kids my age, even the youth group," she confessed. Her brother joined the conversation and admitted that he did too. They had just finished their first year of online high school, and it had been tough in a different way than public school.

They struggled with loneliness the most, and we were already adjusting our plans for the following school year to get them into more co-ops and groups of kids their age.

But I knew in my gut that friends and school changes would never make them feel that they totally belonged. *They were different*—how could they not be? They had witnessed the world's normal up close, and it had changed them. Since that trip Madison had made a commitment to buy and wear only fair-trade or secondhand clothes because she knew that cheap clothes were costing someone their freedom. She had read that cheap clothes often point to slave wages for the world's poorest clothes makers.[4] Jon-Avery was giving free archery lessons to kids because he had tasted the joy of sharing what he'd been given. Emerson was begging to return to Africa. The fads and trends, silliness, and superficial components of our culture would never truly satisfy my kids again. I knew they would not be changed by our world, but I could see the heartache of raising world changers.

"I feel different too," I confessed, and I shared some of my own heartbreak with them. The cost is high, but the payoff is life changing. We cannot forget Veronica's question to my daughter Madison at the start of this book. It has shaped how we want to raise our kids and spend the rest of our lives. I believe every family should ask themselves this question: *What am I supposed to do with what I've been given?* The answer will always lead to redemption.

Five months after that spring trip with my family, I returned to Kenya. I didn't return alone. I brought most of the Mercy House staff with me because I was desperate for my team to understand the world's normal. We brought a new fair-trade product line to teach, visited the maternity homes, witnessed soul-crushing poverty, and slept crammed on the floor of Maureen's home every night. But the highlight was witnessing the hopeless moms we'd left a few months earlier now standing in front of looms and kilns and learning a new skill so they can provide for their families.

By that time our family had given most of our unexpected money away. Our kids thrilled at the idea of sharing it and the process of disbursing it, but we agreed to keep the details private. Keeping it a secret didn't diminish the happiness a bit; it only enhanced it. Somewhere, somehow along the way in our little family—with all its hiccups and hang-ups, imperfections and impossibilities—we were raising kids who would change the world. They had discovered the beauty of sacrifice and the joy of giving. Yes, the world is changing, but we can change the world by pointing our kids to a God who never changes.

Start
WORLD-CHANGING
CONVERSATIONS
with Your Kids

Ask your family the following questions:

1. What has God given us?
2. Is it a blessing or a test?
3. How can we share what we have with others?

Conclusion

A month after I turned in this manuscript to my publisher, I found myself hunkering down with my family for days in Houston, Texas, as Hurricane Harvey destroyed more than 470,000 homes in my city. Rising water threatened most of us as the storm paused over our city and rain fell for days. In our suburb, forty-five minutes north of Houston, we received thirty-four inches of rain in less than forty-eight hours. As the rain continued we would get up in the middle of the night to see how close it was to our doors and how the roof was holding up at Mercy House. Thankfully, the water drained a little faster than it fell, and we escaped flooding. Many like our family who didn't flood were still trapped in their houses for days due to impassable roads, but it was the thousands who lost everything that captured our hearts. I don't know if it was the ongoing news coverage, the cabin fever, or the gratitude that came from escaping Harvey's worst, but we were desperate to do something to help those who were suffering in Houston. And we weren't alone.

Once we were able to leave our homes, we did so with one thought: Who can we help today? Who needs a meal? Who needs dry clothes? Who needs to be rescued by boat? We turned Mercy House into a collection center where we distributed nonperishable food and diapers to evacuees. Stay-at-home moms made and delivered meals to families stuck in hotels while dads mudded out homes, cutting away damaged sheetrock from floodwaters. We collected and distributed thousands of dollars in gift cards. Texas became an army of world changers. It quickly became nearly impossible to find a place to volunteer or donate to because people had made helping others a top priority.

Madison and Jon-Avery spent days with their youth group moving furniture to higher ground and carrying wheelbarrow loads of wet and ruined sheetrock. They wore masks to protect their bodies from the toxic fumes and gloves to prevent staph infections. Emerson got up every morning and asked, "Who are we helping today?" And it felt normal. My kids weren't special or unique in their serving; they simply asked the question our state was asking: What can I do to serve someone today? It's what you do in a storm.

I believe we are supposed to ask this question every single day. This is the heart of generosity. What can I do today to help someone in need? This is compassion. This is Christianity. I have seen the world's normal and looked into the faces of hopelessness, and I can tell you that there is always someone in need. There is always a storm brewing in someone's life. There is always an opportunity to ask this question because the body of Christ is the world's disaster-relief plan. In the middle of Harvey relief efforts, I wondered if our desperation to do something would dry up with the floodwaters. I was reminded that this question, this compelling motivation to give, shouldn't depend on disaster; it should be our way of life. We were created to share what we've been given.

We have to ask ourselves why we are standing on dry ground when the rest of the world seems to be drowning. What can we give today to help someone else? We simply start with the need in front of us. This is how we lead our families. This is how we raise kids who change the world.

Acknowledgments

To Terrell: As you know, I wrote this book during a very difficult season of burnout. Thank you for showing me what it's like to persevere in the middle of a broken leg and a broken heart. We are stronger because of the brokenness we share. I love you.

To Madison: By the time you read these words, you will be preparing to leave for college. It's hard to believe we are at this crossroads. I love the deepening friendship we share and the way you challenge me to be a better person. You are wildly talented, and I cannot wait to see where you fly. I love you, MC.

To Jon-Avery: Your daily quest for holiness and integrity amazes me. You make me a better person. You've given me an example to pray for when I think about whom your sisters will marry one day. I love you, son. Thank you for changing my world.

To Emerson: Sweet Emmy, you add music to our home. You are passionate and determined. You are brave and confident, and you remind me daily to have courage. I love you. You change my world a little every day.

To my Kenyan family: My world is better because you're in it. You give me daily perspective and make me want to give my all every single day.

To Kara: Having a sister as your best friend is almost too good to be true. I love you. Thank you for being my person.

To my parents: Mom and Dad, thank you for loving and supporting me in every phase and season of my life. I love you so much.

To my in-laws: You raised a world changer and then gave him to me. I love you, and I thank God for you.

To the Mercy House squad: You guys are much more than employees and coworkers—you're friends. Thank you for working so hard to empower women around the globe, for listening and talking me off ledges, for reminding me I'm not a big deal and keeping me humble. I love you guys a whole lot.

To readers at wearethatfamily.com: You may just know me better than anyone, which is kind of a weird and beautiful gift the internet has given us. Thank you for being a part of my world.

To Bill Jensen, my agent: Thank you for all your solid advice and walking this writing road with me.

To the Baker Books team: Thank you for making this entire process easy. I'm excited about all the words we will write together.

Notes

Introduction

1. Mother Teresa, *A Simple Path*, comp. Lucinda Vardey (New York: Random House, 1995), 99.

2. Jim Carrey, "Quotable Quotes," *Reader's Digest*, March 2006, 81.

3. David Platt, https://www.youtube.com/watch?v=aoicm4wnQ4c&feature=player_embedded.

Chapter 1 The Question We Must Ask

1. K. P. Yohannan, *Revolution in World Missions: One Man's Journey to Change a Generation*, English Language ed. (Carrollton, TX: GFA Books, 2009), 83.

2. K. P. Yohannan, *No Longer a Slumdog: Bringing Hope to Children in Crisis* (Carrollton, TX: GFA Books, 2011), 85.

Chapter 2 Jesus

1. John Thornton, *Jesus' Terrible Financial Advice: Flipping the Tables on Peace, Prosperity, and the Pursuit of Happiness* (Chicago: Moody, 2016), 124.

2. Max Lucado, *God Came Near* (Nashville: Word Publishing, 1987), 7.

3. Tom Nelson, *Work Matters: Connecting Sunday Worship to Monday Work* (Wheaton: Crossway, 2011), 90.

4. Thornton, *Jesus' Terrible Financial Advice*, 167.

Chapter 3 When There's Too Much or Not Enough to Go Around

1. Wikipedia, s.v. "North–South Divide," last modified October 16, 2017, 11:54, https://en.wikipedia.org/wiki/North–South_divide.

2. John Piper, *A Hunger for God: Desiring God through Fasting and Prayer* (Wheaton: Crossway, 1997), 25–26.

197

3. J. D. Walt, "The Severe Mercy of a Pre-emptive Judgment," Seedbed Daily Text, October 20, 2016, https://us4.campaign-archive.com/?u=02db73c05fa1c7 c5736358be4&id=b36ea32403&e=bd33d08296.

4. Ann Voskamp, *The Broken Way* (Grand Rapids: Zondervan, 2016), 69.

5. Voskamp, *The Broken Way*, 30.

Chapter 4 Is Our Extra a Blessing or a Test?

1. Mahatma Gandhi, https://www.goodreads.com/quotes/17453-whatever -you-do-will-be-insignificant-but-it-is-very.

2. Randy Alcorn, *The Treasure Principle: Unlocking the Secret of Joyful Giving* (Colorado Springs: Multnomah, 2001), 11.

3. Alexandra Sifferlin, "Why Facebook Makes You Feel Bad about Yourself," *Time*, January 24, 2013, http://healthland.time.com/2013/01/24/why-facebook -makes-you-feel-bad-about-yourself/.

4. Randy Alcorn, *Money, Possessions, and Eternity* (Carol Stream, IL: Tyndale, 2003), 94.

5. Wess Stafford, *Too Small to Ignore: Why the Least of These Matters Most* (New York: Crown Publishing Group, 2010), 107.

6. David Platt, *Radical: Taking Back Your Faith from the American Dream* (Colorado Springs: Multnomah, 2010), 111.

7. Alcorn, *The Treasure Principle*, 75.

8. Platt, *Radical*, 217.

Chapter 5 Giving Our Homes a Generosity Overhaul

1. Martin Luther King Jr., The King Center, April 9, 2013, http://www.theking center.org/blog/mlk-quote-week-all-labor-uplifts-humanity-has-dignity-and-im portance-and-should-be-undertaken.

Chapter 6 The High Cost of Giving Our Lives Away

1. John Piper, "Embrace the Life God Has Given You, Desiring God, March 10, 2017, http://www.desiringgod.org/embrace-the-life-god-has-given-you.

2. David Platt, "IF: Gathering - David Platt - 2016," March 28, 2016, video, 30:42, https://vimeo.com/160686752.

Chapter 7 Why We Keep Paying the Price

1. Catherine Wilson, "Raising a Cheerful Giver: Teaching Children to Give Generously," Focus on the Family (Canada), 2014, http://www.focusonthefam ily.ca/parenting/school-age/raising-a-cheerful-giver-teaching-children-to-give -generously.

2. Timothy L. Smith, "10 Examples of Generosity in the Bible and How to Follow Them," Crosswalk.com, December 12, 2016, https://www.crosswalk.com /church/giving/10-examples-of-generosity-in-the-bible-and-how-to-follow-them .html.

Chapter 8 The Happiest People Alive

1. Jill Suttie and Jason Marsh, "5 Ways Giving Is Good for You," *Greater Good Magazine*, December 13, 2010, http://greatergood.berkeley.edu/article/item /5_ways_giving_is_good_for_you.

2. Colleen Walsh, "Money Spent on Others Can Buy Happiness," *Harvard Gazette*, April 17, 2008, http://news.harvard.edu/gazette/story/2008/04/money -spent-on-others-can-buy-happiness/.

3. Suttie and Marsh, "5 Ways Giving Is Good for You." See also Shankar Vedantam, "If It Feels Good to Be Good, It Might Be Only Natural," *Washington Post*, May 28, 2007, http://www.washingtonpost.com/wp-dyn/content/article/2007 /05/27/AR2007052701056.html.

4. Suttie and Marsh, "5 Ways Giving Is Good for You."

5. Amy Wallace, "New Study Shows It's Better to Give Than to Receive," UPI, February 14, 2017, http://www.upi.com/Health_News/2017/02/14/New-study -shows-its-better-to-give-than-to-receive/1771487098057/.

6. Christian Smith and Hilary Davidson, *The Paradox of Generosity: Giving We Receive, Grasping We Lose* (Oxford: Oxford University Press, 2014), 43.

7. Kevin Leman, *Have a New Kid by Friday* (Grand Rapids: Revell, 2012), 18.

8. J. D. Walt, "Why Sharing Is Not the Answer—And What Is," Seedbed Daily Text, May 9, 2017, https://www.seedbed.com/why-sharing-is-not-the-answer -and-what-is/.

9. Jennie Allen, *Restless* (Nashville: Thomas Nelson, 2014), 124.

Chapter 9 What's Really at Stake?

1. John Piper, *A Sweet and Bitter Providence: Sex, Race, and the Sovereignty of God* (Wheaton: Crossway, 2010), 101–2.

2. Jamieson-Fausset-Brown Bible Commentary (1882), s.v. "Nehemiah 2," accessed August 2, 2016, http://biblehub.com/commentaries/jfb/nehemiah/2.htm.

3. Raechel Myers, "At the King's Gate," *She Reads Truth* (blog), February 5, 2015, http://shereadstruth.com/2015/02/05/kings-gate/.

4. Ann Voskamp, "Why You Are Where You Are: For Such a Time as Now," *Ann Voskamp* (blog), June 18, 2013, http://annvoskamp.com/2013/06/why-you -are-where-you-are-for-such-a-time-as-this/.

5. Ann Voskamp, "How We Could Get to Be the Kind of People the World Needs Right Now," *Ann Voskamp* (blog), October 11, 2016, http://annvoskamp .com/2016/10/how-we-could-get-to-be-the-kind-of-people-the-world-needs -right-now/.

Chapter 10 Storing Our Treasures in Heaven

1. Randy Alcorn, *The Treasure Principle: Unlocking the Secret of Joyful Giving* (Colorado Springs: Multnomah, 2001), 40–41.

2. Randy Alcorn, *Money, Possessions, and Eternity* (Carol Stream, IL: Tyndale, 2003), 45.

3. Randy Alcorn, *Heaven* (Carol Stream, IL: Tyndale, 2004), 128.

4. *An Exposition of the Bible: A Series of Expositions Covering All the Books of the Old and New Testament*, vol. 6 (n.p.: The S.S. Scranton Co, 1907), 622.

5. Alcorn, *Heaven*, 166.

6. Abigail Van Buren, *The Best of Dear Abby* (Kansas City, MO: Andrews McMeel Publishing, 1981).

7. Randy Alcorn, "Our Eternal Home," *Thriving Family*, August/September 2013.

8. Randy Alcorn, *The Treasure Principle*, 31–32.

Chapter 11 A Family Soul-Care Plan

1. David Platt, *Radical: Taking Back Your Faith from the American Dream* (Colorado Springs: Multnomah, 2010), 7.

2. Timothy Keller, "Sabbath Rest," Daily Keller, March 11, 2015, http://daily keller.com/sabbath-rest/.

3. Timothy Keller, *King's Cross: The Story of the World in the Life of Jesus* (New York: Dutton, 2011), 43.

Chapter 12 The Answer

1. "Mother Teresa of Calcutta," Crossroads Initiative, September 4, 2016, https://www.crossroadsinitiative.com/saints/quotes-from-blessed-mother-teresa -of-calcutta/.

2. Richard Stearns, *The Hole in Our Gospel: The Answer That Changed My Life and Might Just Change the World* (Nashville: Thomas Nelson, 2009), 60.

3. David Platt, *Radical*, 111.

4. Simon Parry, "The True Cost of Your Cheap Clothes: Slave Wages for Bangladesh Factory Workers," *Post Magazine*, last updated March 31, 2017, http://www.scmp.com/magazines/post-magazine/article/1970431/true-cost-your -cheap-clothes-slave-wages-bangladesh-factory.

Kristen Welch is a Texas girl, born and raised in the South. She has written about her life on wearethatfamily.com for more than a decade. Over the years Kristen has grown a vast following of moms who identify with her vulnerable and often-inspiring writing.

In 2010, Kristen traveled with Compassion International to Kenya on a blogging trip to write about poverty in a huge slum. That experience turned her world upside down, and as a result she and her family founded a nonprofit called Mercy House Global, which works to empower and disciple impoverished women around the world. Part of that work includes overseeing fair-trade retail stores and the work of Fair Trade Friday, a monthly subscription club that has become Kristen's day job. You can learn more about how this ministry started in Kristen's memoir, *Rhinestone Jesus*. Kristen is also the bestselling author of *Raising Grateful Kids in an Entitled World*, a frequent speaker, and a monthly columnist in *ParentLife* magazine.

Kristen lives with her husband and three children in Texas.